COIN SPLENDOUR

A journey into the past

Dedicated
to
My wife Dhimathi

COIN SPLENDOUR

A journey into the past

PRASANNA RAO BANDELA

ABHINAV PUBLICATIONS

abhinav publications
New Delhi

Fig. 14.14 A copper off-metal-strike presentation piece of The East India Company (obverse) with letter 'C' embedded at the centre. Around 1835 A.D.

First published in India 2003

Publishers
Shakti Malik
Abhinav Publications
E-37, Hauz Khas
New Delhi-110016 (INDIA)
Phones: 6566387, 6562784, 6524658
Fax: 91-11-6857009
e-mail: shakti@nde.vsnl.net.in
website: www.abhinavexports.com

Printed at
D.K. Fine Art Press Pvt. Ltd.
Ashok Vihar, Delhi

Lasertypeset by
S.R. Enterprises
Lajpat Nagar-IV
New Delhi-110024
Phone: 011- 6236663

ISBN 81-7017-427-9

Fig. 14.15 A copper off-metal-strike presentation piece of The East India Company (reverse) with regnal year 20 of Shah Alam and Farukkabad mint mark. Around 1835 A.D.

CONTENTS

HE DIED FOR FREEDOM AND HONOUR
MUNISAMI

ACKNOWLEDGEMENTS

A book on numismatics can never be an original piece of work, without the contribution of innumerable scholars who have devoted their lives studying the ancient coins. To all those numismatists from whom I have compiled this information I am indebted, while I take responsibility for the mistakes, if any.

I am grateful to The Hindu, The Economic Times and The Deccan Chronicle for publishing seven of the articles included in this work.

I admire the editorial skills of my friend Ch. S. Madhava Rao who has kindly sifted the manuscript before it goes to press.

G. Ravi Babu has taken photographs of several coins in my collection and produced excellent pictures with exceptional clarity and finer details. K. Rajni Kanth and B. Anjaneyulu have done a neat job of preparing the manuscript. Their professional skills are highly commendable.

Some photographs of electroplated reproductions of gold coins of Gupta and Vijayanagara empires are provided by Mir Fazaluddin Ali Khan, Keeper of Coins, A.P. State Museum, Hyderabad. I profusely thank him for his earnest interest and kind cooperation.

I am grateful to my beloved wife Dhimathi and my affectionate children Srikanth, Sridhar and Vandana without whose understanding and constant support this book would not have become a possibility.

Fig. 12.7 The Great War Memorial plaque (WW-I), posthumously awarded to an Indian soldier, Munisami.

TI CLAVDIVS CAESAR AVG P M TR P IMP
GEORGIVS V DEI GRA: BRITT: OMN: REX
R. IMP. HU. BO. REG. M. THERESIA D. G.
GEORGE VI KING EMPEROR
GEORGIVS V DEI GRA: BRITT: OMN: REX

PREFACE

Every coin tells a story. As a piece of historical evidence it is indeed invaluable because it may add a new fact, or a name, or a date to history.

Collecting coins for the sheer pleasure of it is one thing and the curiosity to know the history behind them is another. On the other hand venturing to write about them is entirely different. It is no less a courageous adventure for any coin collector.

This difficult task imposes several constraints within which one is compelled to work on: coins representing various kingdoms may not be there in one's collection; if available, they may not be in good condition; and published literature and catalogues may not be easily accessible. Lack of knowledge of Persian on my part is another serious handicap that imposes certain restrictions. In view of the difficulties to be encountered, it is imperative to adopt a certain amount of flexibility in setting the limits for the subject matter. Under the circumstances it has become a deliberate choice to cover a few prominent Indian kingdoms upto fifteenth century A.D.

Part of the motivation for this book comes from the desire to consolidate my published articles. Seven of them that appeared in national dailies are included and seven more new essays are written. Sixty photographs of the coins and medals are included. Detailed description is given under each coin and medal, giving transliterations and translations of coin legends. Approximate period to which the coins belong is indicated.

In so far as medals are concerned the description is confined to some classic medals of historical importance, that were issued prior to Indian independence. Here availability of the medals dictated the choice of discussion. Some coin rarities are discussed in the last two chapters. The examples are entirely drawn from my personal collection.

Throughout the book the historical importance of coins is highlighted; and the need for preserving ancient coins as part of our cultural heritage is underlined. I hope this small book will stimulate the reader's interest in the collection and study of ancient coins.

Hyderabad
24 May, 2000

PRASANNA RAO BANDELA

(on Page 1)
Fig. 14.2 A coin of Lysimachus (reverse) with the image of goddess Athena. 306 B.C. (a modern imitation).

(on Page 2)
Fig. 14.1 A coin of Lysimachus (obverse) with deified image of Alexander the Great wearing the horn of Ammon. 306 B.C. (a modern imitation).

(on Page 8)
Fig. 1.5 A variety of ancient and modern coins.

LIST OF PHOTOGRAPHS

Fig. 3.4 A silver hemi-drachm of Antialkidas. 2nd Century B.C.
Obverse: Portrait of the king. Legend *Basileos Nikephorou Antialkidou.*
Reverse: Greek god Zeus standing. Legend in Kharoshti script *Maharajasa Jayadharasa Amtialkitasa* "(coin) of the victorious king Antialkidas".

Fig. 3.5 A silver hemi-drachm of Philoxenos. 2nd Century B.C.
Obverse: Portrait of the king. Legend *Basileos Aniketou Philoxinou.*
Reverse: King on horseback. Legend in Kharoshti script *Maharajasa Apadihatasa Philasinasa* "(coin) of the unconquered king Philoxenos".

Fig. 4.1 A copper coin of Vima Kadphises (obverse & reverse). 78–110 A.D.
Obverse: Portrait of the king standing with his head turned left offering with his right hand an altar with Greek legend *Basileon Soter Megas Ooemo Kadphises.*
Reverse: God Siva standing in front of a bull holding a trident in right hand. Legend in Kharoshti script *Maharajasa Rajadhirajasa Sarvaloga Iswarasa Mahiswarasa Vima Kathaphishasa Tradara.*

Fig. 4.2 A copper coin of Huvishka. Probably 162–182 A.D.
Obverse: King reclining on a cushion with the sceptre in raised left hand with the legend *Shao Nano Shao Oeshki Koshano.*
Reverse: God standing left with Greek legend *Miiro.*

Fig. 5.1 Coins of Srimukha Sata, Gauthamiputra Sathakarni, Vashistiputra Pulumavi. 2nd Century B.C. to 2nd Century A.D.
Obverse: With the legends *Srimukasata, Siri Satakanisa, Siri Pulumavisa.*

Fig. 5.2 Coins of Srimukha Sata, Gauthamiputra Sathakarni, Vashistiputra Pulumavi.
Reverse: With Ujjain symbol.

Fig. 5.3 Potin and lead coins of Sathavahana period with Ujjain symbol. 2nd Century B.C. to 2nd Century A.D.

Fig. 5.4 Lead coins of the Maharathis, the feudatories of Sathavahanas.
Obverse: An elephant facing left with Brahmi legends *Maharathisa* and *Maharathisa Sivakhadasa.* 2nd Century A.D.

Fig. 5.5 Lead coins of the Maharathis, the feudatories of Sathavahanas.
Reverse: A Buddhist tree in railing. 2nd Century A.D.

Fig. 11.1 A medal of East India Company (obverse) with Shah Alam's regnal year 19, and Murshidabad mint mark. Around 1835 A.D.

Fig. 11.2 A medal of East India Company (reverse).

Fig. 12.1 British War Medal, Victory Medal (WW-I) and Burma Medal (obverse).

Fig. 12.2 British War Medal (WW-I), Victory Medal and Burma Medal (reverse).

Fig. 12.3 Delhi Coronation Durbar Medal, The Defence Medal (WW-II) and Independence of India Medal (obverse).

Fig. 12.4 Delhi Coronation Durbar Medal, The Defence Medal (WW-II) and Independence of India Medal (reverse).

Fig. 12.5 Commemorative Medal of Queen Victoria's Hanover visit 1837 (obverse) with uncrowned head of the Queen.

Fig. 12.6 Commemorative Medal of Queen Victoria's Hanover visit 1837 (reverse) with St. George riding a horse.

Fig. 12.7 The Great War Memorial plaque (WW-I), posthumously awarded to an Indian soldier, Munisami.

Fig. 13.1 Coins struck on different metals other than the one used for regular issues (obverse).

Fig. 13.2 Coins struck on different metals other than the one used for regular issues (reverse).

Fig. 14.1 A coin of Lysimachus (obverse) with deified image of Alexander the Great wearing the horn of Ammon. 306 B.C. (a modern imitation).

Fig. 14.2 A coin of Lysimachus (reverse) with the image of goddess Athena. 306 B.C. (a modern imitation).

Fig. 14.3 A potin coin of Srimukha Sata with Sanskrit legend *Srimuka Sata* (obverse) and faint Ujjain symbol (reverse). 3rd Century B.C.

Fig. 14.4 A silver coin of Kuninda.
Obverse: With the Sanskrit legend *Rajna Kunindasa Amoghabhuthasa Maharajasa.*
Reverse: Same legend in Kharoshti script.

Fig. 14.5 A coin of Tiberius Caesar with the legend TI. CLAVDIVS CAESAR. AVG. PM. TRP. IMP. and the portrait of the king (obverse). 1st Century A.D. (a fake coin).

1. INTRODUCTION*

There is nothing like money that attracts man. More so, when it takes the form of coins of glittering gold and sparkling silver. They were as greedily sought after for their value as they were readily parted to secure more desirable things in this world. No wonder, they dictated the destinies of men for centuries.

Even when out of circulation they retain their intrinsic worth because of the precious metal contained in them. On the other hand, they attract the attention of coin collectors who clamour to own them for their rarity and beauty. Some of them are so cute that they are highly fascinating.

Let us consider for example three silver rupees of East India Company (Fig. 1.2) and two gold coins, one each of Gupta Empire (Fig. 1.3) and Vijayanagara Empire (Fig. 1.4). They are no longer the legal currency in India, yet they are scarce. The special charm of these enchanting pieces would certainly beckon a second glance. In all probability, one would like to see the real ones, if not tempted to possess them at any cost.

What exactly is a coin? It is a small bit of metal, an embodiment of money, used in exchange or trade. It is generally circular in shape with a few exceptions. It tends to be relatively thin in proportion to its diameter. It contains inscriptions as to who made it, what its exchange value is and when it was made. It includes generally an image of a ruler or an eminent person or an emblem of national importance.

In the ancient times, before money as a means of exchange was invented, people resorted to barter system of trading. In course of time, many things served as units of money: animals—cows, oxen, sheep; articles of daily consumption—bottles of gin, dried fish, groundnuts, palm kernels, palm oil, ruffia fibre, sweet potatoes, tea bricks, tobacco balls; implements of daily use—axe-heads, fish hooks, spades, throwing knives; and many curious things—bracelets of

*Courtesy: The Deccan Chronicle. This article was published by the author under the title 'Coin Splendour' in The Deccan Chronicle dated 19-2-1995.

elephant's tail hair, cowries, feathers, glass beads, metal pieces of odd shapes (Fig. 1.1), necklaces of shells, and whale teeth.

The need for convenient form of money to facilitate economic transactions was recognised by the Chinese as early as 10,000 BC. Originally, they used agricultural implements such as knife and spade as medium of exchange, but later they used miniature copies of these tools instead of the real ones. Over a period of time these tool-shaped pieces of bronze developed into a kind of currency. They are variously known as 'chi-knife money' (chi-tao), 'pu-spade money and bridge money'.

The coin money in the modern sense was invented around 620–600 BC in ancient Lydia in Asia Minor (now part of Western Turkey). These coins introduced by King Croseus were round metal pieces. They were struck and carried designs. They had relatively high value for their weight. They were also easier to carry and use. Soon, the usage of coins as money spread to other countries.

Fig. 1.2 Silver rupees of East India Company with the heads of William IV and Victoria, 1835 and 1840.

The rise and fall of the great early civilisations of Greece and Rome are well chronicled and illustrated in their coins. The gold coins of Guptas in India reveal the grandeur of their golden age. They witness the flowering and decay of artistic expression of their times. Many traces of human development can also be seen on them. They reflect the technological progress in tools and dies that were used to mint (and counterfeit) them. In fact, they are intimately connected with the larger story of man.

For the historian, every coin is a bit of history in metal. Coins can tell us who we were, what we did, and what we thought and held as beautiful over the centuries. Every ancient coin therefore has the potential to reveal clues to the unanswered questions about our ancestors. There is a body of knowledge called numismatics which aims to study coins with a view to reconstructing history.

Fig. 1.1 Metal pieces of odd shapes marked with symbols, used as money in ancient times. 6th to 3rd Century B.C.

Fig. 1.3 A gold coin of Chandra Gupta Vikramaditya.
Obverse: The king standing left, holding a bow in left hand and an arrow in the right hand. Garuda standard on the left. *Chandra* below the left arm. Legend: *Devasri Maharajadhiraja Sri Chandragupta*.
Reverse: Goddess Lakshmi seated on a lotus holding a lotus in the left hand and a noose in the right. Legend: *Srivikrama*. 375–413 A.D.

Fig. 1.4 A gold coin of Vijayanagara. 1336 A.D.

The Latin word for a coin is *numisma* and a collector of coins is called *numismatist*. Coin collection is one of the most popular hobbies in the world. One can derive a lot of recreation and joy in forming a collection and the interest and knowledge it brings. In the West, coins are acquired for another purpose. Some investors buy rare coins that appreciate in value, only to sell at a later date to make a profit. Since there is no such market in India today coins are collected here mostly for pleasure.

It is difficult for any person to collect all the coins of the world. Therefore, it is prudent to specialise in one or two areas: Ancient India; East India Company; British India; Modern India; any other country such as the United States of America. Depending on time, energy and money available endless themes can be taken up: coins with ships, trees, animals, famous men and women etc. Mint rarities could be another area: proofs, uncirculated coins, off-metal-strikes, mint errors or rejects and even counterfeits.

Coins have been with us for several thousand years. Even after the introduction of paper currency, cheques and credit cards, they are not abandoned altogether. They still render their humble service as the most durable small change. And they will almost certainly be around for the foreseeable future. And that is good news for coin lovers.

Fig. 2.1 Square and round punch-Marked silver Karsapanas of ancient times weighing 32 *ratis* each. 5th to 3rd Century B.C.

2. MAURYAN LEGACY*

The origin of coinage in India is shrouded in mystery. In ancient times, gold dust washed down the Indus and other rivers served as high currency. Herodotus in his "Clio" tells us that when an Indian satrapy was included in the Achaemenid empire of Persia between 518 B.C. and 350 B.C., 360 talents, approximately 3 kg of gold dust, was paid annually as tribute from the province into the royal treasury. Silver from natural resources, not available in plenty in India, was obtained in large quantities in exchange for gold, which was cheaper here than elsewhere in the world.

The earliest known coins of value dating back to 600 B.C. were small ingots of silver marked with three circular dots; and some heavy bent bars with a punch on one side. These were not found in great quantities.

There are references to panas or karsapanas in Kautilya's Arthasastra and Manu's Dharmasastra. These were simply punch-marked coins or Dharanas or Puranas and were found throughout the country from Takshasila to Raj Shahi (Bangladesh) and from Behat (Saharanpur, U.P.) to Coimbatore (Tamil Nadu).

According to Quintus Curtius, Omphis (Ambi, an Indian king) presented "Signati Argenti LXXX Talenta"—80 talents (680 gm) of stamped silver—to Alexander the Great. Such was the status of silver for a royal tribute. These and other pieces of evidence reveal that punch-marked coins were well established during the fourth and third centuries B.C.

The shape, form and weight of these punch-marked coins suggest that they are indigenous, with no foreign influence. A punch-marked piece of metal was a natural development of a paper hundi or note of hand. It is probable that in India, as in Lydia, coins had originally been struck by goldsmiths or silversmiths or private merchants or guilds (seni). Subsequently the royal seal of authority must have been added to the already existing marks.

---

*Courtesy: The Hindu. This article was published by the author under the title 'Mauryan legacy' in The Hindu dated 12-8-1990.

According to the nail-mark theory, these punch marks are stamps of authority to guarantee a certain quantum of precious metal of recognised weight and fineness. Long before the emergence of these coins, this marking was thought to have been done in a simple way. A nail of bronze or any hard metal was cut and broken into two halves and the upper part used as a punch. A sharp blow with a hammer impressed the nail mark on a piece of metal. It is not unlikely that any two nails, cut and broken through, would produce the same profile and thus make exactly the same mark on the metal. Then came the transition from a broken nail to a predesigned punch with a recognisable symbol.

Fig. 2.2 Punch marked silver Karsapanas and a copper coin with the Mauryan Royal symbol of three arched chaitya. 5th to 3rd Century B.C.

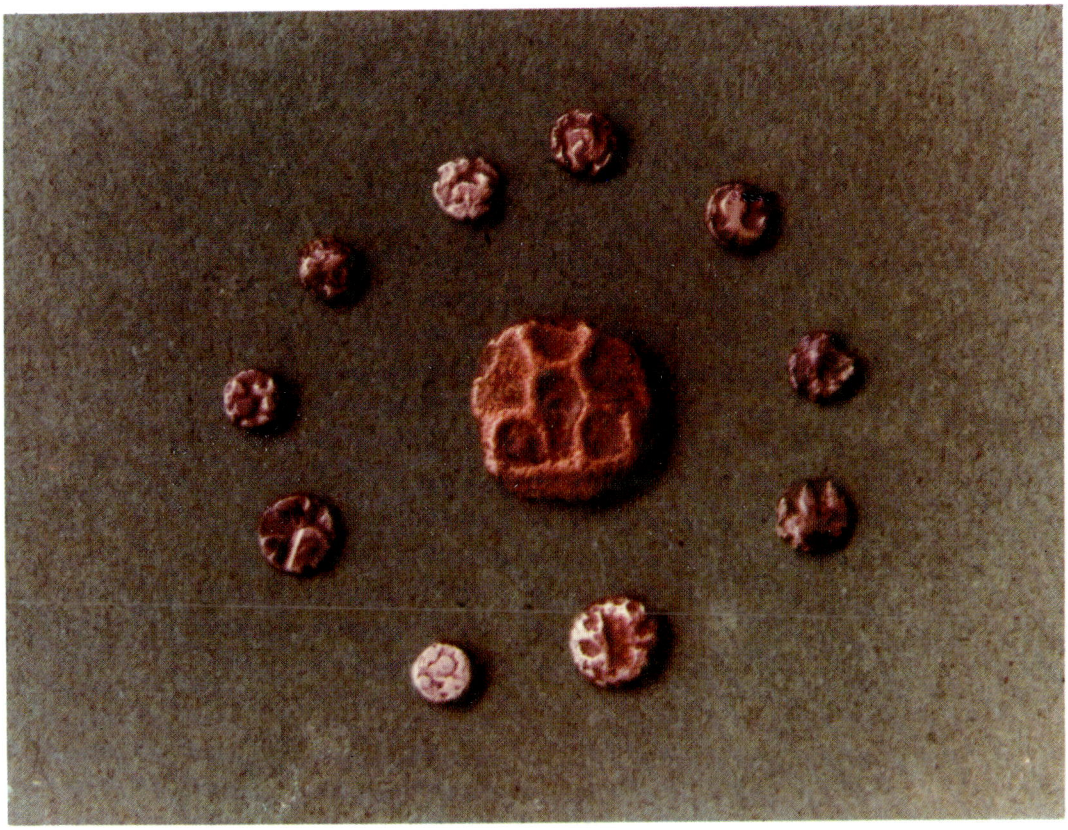

Fig. 2.3 Masakas, the tiny silver coins of Mauryan period each weighing 2 *ratis*. 5th to 3rd Century B.C.

Punch-marked coins are rectangular or circular flat pieces of thin silver cut from a hammered sheet of metal and clipped to proper weight (Fig. 2.1, 2.2). Their weights vary from 48 to 53 grains. This is attributed to loss of metal during circulation, estimated between 0.016 to 0.025 gm for every 10 years. According to a scholar, the standard weight of a coin is 32 ratis or 57 grains. Gen. Sir A. Cunningham estimated the weight of a standard silver coin at 58.56 grains (the average weight of one gunja berry—rati—is 1.83 grains). It is quite surprising how the weight of 100 panas should almost equal one pound Troy (5,760 grains). It may have been due to the Greek influence in the Mauryan empire, with the presence of a Greek ambassador Megasthenes in the court of Chandragupta Maurya. Such parity in weights and measures must have been of immense value for East-West trade.

Most of these silver coins are alloyed with copper. Some having 72 to 80 per cent of the precious metal are said to belong to the pre-Mauryan period, and others with 68.5 to 79 per cent to the Mauryan period. It is possible to classify the coins on the basis of their fabric—thin, medium, thick, round, rectangular, clipped or unclipped and the symbols on the obverse and reverse. Several varieties may be segregated and a reliable chronological order arrived at. Rectangular coins are said to be older than the circular ones; and coins with marks on one side are older than those marked on both sides.

The symbols on the obverse are varied. Some minute indistinct marks are seen on the reverse and identification poses a problem. Some are only partly visible, probably due to the blow of the hammer on one side of the punch head, resulting in partial impressions. Sometimes they appear jumbled as if superimposed, one over the other, on the limited space apparently imprinted at different times, indicating the chequered career of each piece. Simple or complex patterns emerged: ornamental circles or wheels, the sun, human figures, animals—bull, elephant, horse, deer, rhinoceros, fish, crocodile and tortoise—bow and arrow, hills and trees. Over 300 varieties have been identified.

A scholar tells us about one symbol which helps us in fixing the period of these coins. A crescent on the three-arched hill or chaitya on a copper coin was first seen on the Sohagaura copper plate of the Mauryan period. It was also seen on a sandstone pillar excavated at Kumrahar (Patna), and on terracotta dishes of the Mauryan period found at Bulandibagh (Patna). These evidences suggest that it was the imperial mark of the Mauryans. Since this is often seen on punch-marked coins, we can safely assign them to the Mauryan period—third or fourth century B.C.

Masaka: Throughout the Mauryan empire the punch-marked coin or the pana was one standard unit of silver currency. Kautilya's Arthasastra has an account of four denominations of silver coins issued by many mints of the Mauryan empire. There were an ardha pana (1/2 pana), a pada (1/4 pana), and an ardha pada or ashta bhaga (1/8 pana). Another denomination, the masaka (1/16 pana) also existed (Fig. 2.3).

The masaka has the distinction of being the first ever one-sixteenth unit of a standard silver currency issued on Indian soil. It is exceedingly rare and that is what makes it a collector's prized possession. It derives its name from 'masa', a bean variety (*Caesalpina bonduc*), which was used in ancient times as a standard unit of weight for estimating the value of precious stones and metals. Another seed, the 'rati' of the gunja creeper *Abrus precatorius* is still popular in various parts of India. While a rati (raktika) served as the lowest denomination of weight, masa was the next highest. While the silver masa is equal to two ratis, a copper masa weighs five. These two masas were regarded as units, 16 of each respectively constituted the weight of a standard silver coin (32 ratis) and that of a standard copper coin (80 ratis). These two masas were prevalent during the period represented by orthodox law-books like the Code of Manu. Later different masas of other values (6, 10, 12 or 16 ratis) were also in use in different parts of India. The silver masaka, with a standard weight of two ratis, remained in circulation as the lowest unit of silver currency for over five centuries.

This diminutive beauty is circular, about the size of a gunja berry, measuring 4 to 6 mm across and weighing two ratis (3.6 grains or 0.23 gm). Most of them were made by the die-striking process and as the space on the coin was extremely limited, it could not afford several punches. Even the impression of a single symbol is not very clear.

A metal piece was first made to conform to the correct weight of two ratis and heated in a furnace. It was then flattened by stamping with a mark of authority. The weight of 16 masakas was equal to one silver pana (32 ratis) for universal acceptance of its exchange value. Attainment of such high standards of excellence is quite remarkable.

In the picture are nine masakas and one ardha pada from the author's cabinet. The average weight of the masaka is 0.2 gm; and their width ranges between 4.5 and 6 mm. The ardha pada measures 9.5 mm across and weighs 0.43 gm. The weight of these coins must have been reduced by the loss of metal during their circulation.

One masaka is carefully punch-marked, showing a tree with an animal facing right. The remaining are die-struck coins. Symbols on five of them are identifiable: a triskeles, a fish, a tortoise, and a taurine to the right of something. Marks on the other three are not clear. A two-arched chaitya, probably part of a three-arched one, is seen on the ardha pada. While the reverse is blank in all cases, the symbols on the obverse are similar to those found on punch-marked panas.

The coins might have been royal emblems, mint marks, symbols of worship or stamps of private merchants or guilds (seni). As they defy any interpretation, their significance is not clear.

Fig. 3.1 A coin of Lysimachus with deified image of Alexander the Great wearing the horn of Ammon. 306 B.C. (a modern imitation).

3. COMING OF THE YAVANAS

The mysterious land beyond the Hindu Kush with its lush green valleys entertained the fantasies of Asian nomads since time immemorial. Cattle-grazing pastoral communities from Central Asia settled in Indus valley as early as 1500 BC. A millennium later Yavanas, Sakas and Pahlavas (Greeks, Scythians and Parthians) established small kingdoms there. Achaemenid king Darius the Great annexed Gandhara to Persian empire in 518 BC. Alexander the Great of Macedonia invaded India in 327 BC (Fig. 3.1). Detailed account of the story was colourfully narrated by ancient writers like Arrian, Diodorus, Trogus and Plutarch, as well as modern historians like McCrindle.

Awed by the 120,000 strong force led by Alexander several Indian princes, like Ambi of Taxila, welcomed the conqueror and surrendered, but brave kings like Porus did not submit until the invader proved his mettle face-to-face in the battle. This was said to be Alexander's last great battle which he won. He founded two cities Nicaea (to celebrate his victory) and Bucephala (named after his horse Bucephalus which died there). On the Hyphasis (Beas) river he erected 12 altars one each for the Olympian gods. But for the refusal of his weary soldiers to move further in the tropical rains, Alexander might well have advanced to the land of the Ganges, and India might have been as profoundly affected by Greek civilisation as was the Middle East.

When Alexander died in 323 BC his last two representatives returned home leaving Chandra Gupta Maurya to annex Punjab and Gandhara. Determined to regain Indian provinces to Greek fold, Seleucus Nicator, a former general of Alexander, then ruling the lands between Babylon and India, invaded Punjab in 322 BC only to face defeat. As a result he ceded to Magadha all the lands in trans-Indus region—Kabul, Herat, Kandahar and Baluchistan. A marriage alliance was settled between the two royal families, and ambassadors were exchanged. Later, Bindusara was in touch with Antiochus I, son of Seleucus; and his son Asoka strengthened and maintained diplomatic and trade relations with all his Western neighbours—Antiochus II Theos of Syria, Ptolemy II Philadelphus of Egypt, Antigonus II Gonatas of Macedonia, Magas of Cyrene and Alexander of Epirus.

Towards the end of third century BC, the Mauryan empire was in a state of disintegration. Antiochus III crossed the Hindu Kush in 207 BC with war elephants; but having come to friendly terms with Sophagasenos (Soubhuti) he returned with still more elephants. At this time, the Seleucid kingdom was also crumbling, when Arsaces I and Diodotus, governors of Parthia and Bactria, declared independence. Later, Demetrios, son of Euthydemos, extended the Bactrian state deep into Punjab only to witness some of his conquests, Kabul and Taxila, and Bactria itself fall to a rival Eukratides. Henceforth there were two independent States in the region of Gandhara. The principal rulers of the house of Euthydemos were Apollodotus, Menander (Fig. 3.2, 3.3), Strato I, Zoilos and Hippostratos; and those of the line of Eukratides were Heliokles, Antialkidas (Fig. 3.4, 3.5), and Hermaios. In 58 BC, Scythian invaders under Maues (or Moga) established their rule in Pushkalavathi (Peshawar) thus creating a wedge between the two Greek kingdoms in Gandhara and in 40 BC, the Bactrian rulers at Kabul were replaced by Parthian invaders under Vonones.

Soon there were so many princes of foreign origin simultaneously ruling in Gandhara and Indus regions that it is difficult to construct their genealogy or chronology. There is hardly any evidence of inscriptions or books, to help in this regard. We come to know more about them from Col. Todd's discovery in 1824, that Greek coins had once been struck in India. Names of 33 Greek and 26 Indo-Scythian and Indo-Parthian princes were recovered from coin-legends. Not more than 6 are known from other sources. Thus these coins alone are responsible for the recovery of a whole period of Indian history relating to Indus region. The extreme rarity of the coins of a few kings like Apollophanes, Polyxeons, Theophilos leads us to suppose that they were pretenders or feudatories. The most important Bactrian kings judging from their coins were Antialkidas, Apollodotus, Menander, Stratos and Hippostratos.

Early coins of Bactrians resemble those issued by other kings of the Greek world. The beautiful gold staters minted in Bactria by Diodotus, Euthydemos and Eukratides were current in Gandhara. They were the first gold coins to circulate on Indian soil. Most of the coins issued in Gandhara were of silver and copper. Nickel coins were issued for the first time ever, by two princes Pantaleon and Agathokles. Remarkably, each territory began minting square coins in bronze and silver. Square coinage is fairly common in India as early as sixth century BC but its adoption by the Greek rulers in Gandhara affords a significant evidence of the penetration of eastern influences into western culture. As one scholar put it, "many of the coins of this region are indeed perfect examples of cultural hybrids".

Fig. 3.2 A silver hemi-drachm of Menander. 2nd Century B.C.
Obverse: Portrait of the king. Greek legend *Basileos Soteros Menandrou.*
Reverse: Greek goddess Pallas standing. Legend in Kharoshti script *Maharajasa tratasa Menandrasa.* "(coin) of the king, the saviour, Menander".

In the Greek tradition they are die-struck, have inscriptions and feature gods. These features are entirely new and introduced for the first time in India. On the other hand they may be square in Indian tradition, and have inscriptions in Prakrit using Kharoshti script. The double-die-striking was certainly novel to India. Now the coins showed not only greater symmetry of shape but also an advance in the art of die-cutting; the devices entirely Greek must have been engraved by Greeks or Indians trained in Greek tradition, who displayed greater flexibility.

For the first time in India silver coinage with the portraits of the king was introduced by the Indo-Bactrians, following their Greek contemporaries. The effigies were boldly drawn to indicate realistic figure of the king. Generally diademed or helmeted bust is presented. Some of the kings are seen with 'Two Piloi' (caps) of Dioskouroi or a 'Kausia' (a flat cap). Demetrios fancied wearing the Indian elephant head-dress. Sometimes the busts of two rulers were depicted on the same obverse. Around the portraits there is a Greek inscription which usually has three parts. The first is Basileon (The king); the second is his title such as Soteros, Megalou, Antiketou, Nikepokorou, Philpatros, Epiphanou, Dikaiou; and lastly these two are followed by the name of the king.

On the reverse a Greek god or goddess, such as Apollo, Artemis, Dioskouroi, Herakles, is depicted. Another novelty is the appearance of monograms formed of Greek letters. For the first time ever, Prakrit translation of Greek inscriptions

Fig. 3.3 A silver hemi-drachm of Apollodotus. 2nd Century B.C.
Obverse: Portrait of the king. Legend *Basileos Soteros Apollodotou.*
Reverse: Greek goddess Pallas standing. Legend in Kharoshti script *Maharajasa tratasa Apaladatasa* "(coin) of the king, the saviour, Apollodotus".

in Kharoshti script was provided on the reverse (Fig. 3.3, 3.5). They read like *Maharajasa Jayadharasa* (Coin of victorious king) *Amtialkitasa, Maharajasa Apadihatasa* (Coin of the unconquered king) *philasinasa* and *Maharajasa Tratasa* (Coin of the great king, saviour) *Menandrasa.*

The coinage of Indo-Greek kings made a deep impression on their successors. Saka princes while adopting many Greek features employed a characteristic coinage of their own. Parthian influence is also seen particularly in the title *Basileos Basileon* (King of Kings) which all these kings inscribed on their coins.

Fig. 3.4 A silver hemi-drachm of Antialkidas. 2nd Century B.C.
Obverse: Portrait of the king. Legend *Basileos Nikephorou Antialkidou.*
Reverse: Greek god Zeus standing. Legend in Kharoshti script *Maharajasa Jayadharasa Amtialkitasa* "(coin) of the victorious king Antialkidas".

Fig. 3.5 A silver hemi-drachm of Philoxenos. 2nd Century B.C.
Obverse: Portrait of the king. Legend *Basileos Aniketou Philoxinou.*
Reverse: King on horseback. Legend in Kharoshti script *Maharajasa Apadihatasa Philasinasa* "(coin) of the unconquered king Philoxenos".

Maues was the first Saka king to have ruled in Punjab. His silver coins are not plentiful. The finest type has a 'biga', a two-horsed chariot, on the obverse. His copper coins show an elephant on the obverse and a caduceus (staff of a god Hermes) on the reverse. On another issue, the king is depicted on horseback. Silver coins of later kings Azes I and Azilises are in plenty. As on Maues coinage, Greek gods, such as Dioskouroi, Herakles, Pallas, Poseiden and Zeus, appear on their coinage. They introduced for the first time the Indian goddess Lakshmi on their coinage. The commonest type of Azes I shows a bull on the obverse and a lion on the reverse. Sometimes, he is shown sitting cross-legged in Indian fashion.

The earliest known Pahlava king was Vonones. It appears that while he was ruling in Parthia, eastern satrapies were ruled by members of his family. This perhaps was the reason why on most of the coins found in Punjab his name appears conjointly with either that of his brother Spalahores, or his nephew Spalagadames. On some other coins names of the latter two princes appear, together. Spalarises struck coins of his own; and also conjoined with Azes II. All his coins show 'the king on horse' symbol. The most important of the later Pahlava kings is Gondophares or Gondopharnes. He was famous as the king of India, often mentioned in the traditional stories associated with the apostle St. Thomas. Most of his drachms are of billon. His copper coins show the king's bust on the obverse and the Greek gods Pallas and Nike on the reverse. The same type is issued by the later kings—Abdagases, Orthagnes and Pakores.

And it would seem probable that the tribes who invaded India included diverse elements which mingled indistinguishably together so that it is not possible to assert that one dynasty is definitely Pahlava while another is Saka.

With the coming of Yavanas, the trade between India and Western world improved remarkably. The trade route from Taxila went to Kabul and Kandahar linking up with the routes across Persia to Black Sea ports and eastern Mediterranean. The central Asian route connecting China with Bactria, soon to become famous as the 'old silk route', brought Chinese goods into India. Indian merchants established trade missions en route at several places, such as Kashgar, Yarkand, Khotan, Miran, Kucha, Karashahar and Turfan. Alexandria-Kapisu-Bagram, a city north of Kabul founded by Alexander, became a clearing house for India's western trade. It flourished so much that the tax levied on foreign trade became an important source of income for the Mauryan empire.

Interchange of ideas, mostly religious, appears to have been considerable. This is more evident from an erudite Buddhist text Milinda Panha (The Questions of Milinda) written in the form of dialogues between King Menander and philosopher Nagasena, as a result of which the king had accepted Buddhism. Again from an inscription of second century BC, at Besnagar (Bhilsa Dist., MP), it was known that Heliodoros, envoy of king Antialkidas of Taxila, has recorded his conversion to Vaishnava Vasudeva sect. On the other hand Megasthenes, the Greek ambassador at the court of Chandra Gupta Maurya, has recorded his impressions of our country in *The Indica* through which India was introduced to the western world.

The most visible impact could be seen in Gandhara art, a distinguished school developed at Taxila. It depicted Indian themes in Graeco-Roman style of Alexandrian art. This style is visible in its idealized representation of Buddha with youthful Apollo-like face, sometimes in Roman imperial robes. Thus, Gandhara became the confluence of various cultural influences, where the Indian mysticism appears to have been clad in the Greek beauty of form, while Eastern feeling ran through the Western moulds.

Fig. 4.1 A copper coin of Vima Kadphises (obverse & reverse). 78–110 A.D.
Obverse: Portrait of the king standing with his head turned left offering with his right hand an altar with Greek legend *Basileon Soter Megas Ooemo Kadphises.*
Reverse: God Siva standing in front of a bull holding a trident in right hand. Legend in Kharoshti script *Maharajasa Rajadhirajasa Sarvaloga Iswarasa Mahiswarasa Vima Kathaphishasa Tradara.*

4. THE KUSHANAS

The Kushanas were one of the four great Eurasian powers during the first three centuries of the Christian era, comparable to Rome, China and Parthia. Their ruling line descended from a Central Asian nomadic people called Yueh-Chih who inhabited the Kansu province of North-Western China during the second century BC.

Kujula Kadphises (Kiu-siu-kio) united all the five tribes of Yueh-Chih under the banner of his Kushana (Kuei-Shuang) tribe, and established the Kushana empire around 135 BC that extended into India. In one of his coin-legends he proudly describes himself as a Kushana leader (Kushana Yuasa or Yavugasa). On one copper coin of Hermaios, the last Indo-Bactrian ruler, the name of Kujula Kadphises appears on the reverse. It is known that Kujula (Kuyula or Kusula) was a title used by the ruling families of Taxila. This suggests that he was initially a tributary of Bactrian Greeks. Later he overwhelmed the Pahlavas then ruling in Kabul valley and conquered Afghanistan; and he extended his rule to Gandhara and lower Swat valley in the North-Western India. His son Vima Kadphises annexed Taxila deposing the last Pahlava prince Pakores and extended the kingdom to northern India.

Kanishka (Kaneshko or Kaneshki), who may have belonged to another branch of Yueh-Chih, was a great ruler of this dynasty. His accession is believed to be between 78 and 144 AD. Having subjugated all the Sakas and Pahlavas in the North-Western India he further extended his empire that covered a large territory. It stretched from Bukhara (now Uzbek, USSR) in the west to Patna in the Ganges valley in the east; and from Pamirs (now Tadzik, USSR) in the north to central India in south as far as the Vindhyas. The kingdom reached its zenith during his rule that lasted 23 years; and it continued to prosper under his son Huvishka. But the Kushana rule after Vasudeva gradually disintegrated, though their descendants held the Kabul valley till 425 AD.

The Kushanas certainly imitated their Parthian predecessors in many respects. They adopted the previous system of government by means of Ksatrapas who functioned as their governors and later as hereditary sub-kings. And they used the same or similar titles such as *Basileus Basileon* (King of Kings).

Prior to Kushana invasion of India there was a great intercourse between Romans and the Yueh-Chih; and it resulted in the Kushana ambassadors being actually sent to the court of Roman emperor Augustus. Exports from India to different provinces of Roman empire were carried by sea from the south and over land routes in the north. A major branch of the famous Silk Road that carried Indian luxury goods to Rome and China passed through Afghanistan where a transhipment centre existed at Balkh. Indian merchants established trade missions en route at several places such as Kashgar, Yarkand, Khotan, Miran, Kucha, Karashahar and Turfan. Their trade had flourished so much that Kapisu-Bagram, the summer capital of Kushanas, became a clearing house for Indian goods. The resultant prosperity of the Kushanas was reflected in the introduction in abundance of 'denarius', the Kushana gold stater which was similar to the Roman 'aureus'.

Fig. 4.2 A copper coin of Huvishka. Probably 162–182 A.D.
Obverse: King reclining on a cushion with the sceptre in raised left hand with the legend *Shao Nano Shao Oeshki Koshano.*
Reverse: God standing left with Greek legend *Miiro.*

Minting of a large number and variety of gold coins was the unique feature of Kushana rulers. In fact, the first ever gold coin minted on Indian soil was that of the second ruler Vima Kadphises. His gold coinage followed the standard of the Roman 'aureus' of 124 grains, which was then popular in most of the Asian countries; but the Kushana 'denarius' weighed a little less at 123.2 grains (8 gm). Vima also issued double staters, but they were discontinued by the later rulers. All the rulers also issued 'quarter denarius' that weighed 30.8 grains (2 gm).

Their silver coinage was scarce, mainly because of world shortage of silver in those days. Kujula Kadphises is known to have minted at Ta-Hsia (Eastern Bacteria) some small obols weighing 11.2 grains (0.725 gm). Hemi-drachms, called 'drammas' weighing around 32 grains, were occasionally issued by Vima, Huvishka and Vasudeva.

Kushana copper coinage on the other hand was abundant; and it was issued in three varieties, pana, half-pana and quarter-pana. The highest denomination pana weighed 260 grains (16.848 gm). The Kushana rulers were credited for adjusting the weight of copper coinage to the changing rates between gold and copper; and the successive rulers appear to have reduced the weight of the subsequent copper issues along with the gold coinage.

The obverse of Kushana coinage is represented by a general theme of the king offering a sacrifice at a small round altar. This Zoroastrian Mazdean motif is basic to their coinage. It resembles the bas-relief carved on a boulder near the Darius' relief at Bisutan and similar ones at Tang-i-Sarwak. Sacrifice over a flame is an essential act of the Vedic religion of India as well as that of Zoroastrian faith. This motif reinforces the Indo-Iranian religious beliefs, and it symbolizes religious integration; but it was, however, abandoned by later rulers. Though the royal bust above the clouds or rocks is a frequent emblem, several other varieties also appeared. The king is depicted in various postures: riding on an elephant, reclining on a couch, seated cross-legged in Indian fashion, seated with arms raised, seated on a throne, or seated on a two-horsed chariot.

As with Indo-Bactrian coinage, the Kushana coinage also depicted gods on the reverse but with a significant difference. It featured a great 'mixed multitude' of gods of Greek, Scythic, Iranian and Indian religions. The natural explanation for this diversity is that these various classes of coins were current in different provinces of the large empire, where several religions thrived side by side. These coins, no doubt, reflect the particular form of religion that prevailed in the district in which they were struck. This remarkable eclecticism bears witness to the great religious tolerance and reconciliation of the Kushanas who were ardent followers of Buddhism. If they borrowed Hellenic, Roman and Iranian deities, they equally encouraged the Indian divinities of those days. What is conspicuous is the appearance of the name of the god or goddess on the right flan.

Coin-legends of the early Kushanas are bilingual. The name and the title of the king appear in Greek letters on the obverse; while its Sanskrit translation is placed on the reverse in Kharoshti script. But Kanishka and his followers used only Greek script on both sides. Most of them used the Parthian title of *Basileus Basileon* (King of Kings) while Vima Kadphises preferred the title *Soter Megas* (the great saviour), and Kanishka introduced the Persian title *Shao Nano Shao* (King of Kings).

Following the tradition of Indo-Greeks, the Kushanas also placed emblems on their coins. On most of them, a four-pronged symbol makes its appearance. It looks more like an altar, but its significance is not clear; and with minor variations, its form is specific to a particular king. There are one or two exceptions, like the presence of a 'Nandipada' (the hoof-mark of a bull), the sacred symbol of Saivism, as can be seen on the coins of Vima Kadphises. These marks are very helpful for the assignment of a coin to a particular king.

Presented here are two copper coins, of Vima Kadphises and Huvishka (Fig. 4.1, 4.2). Both of them are panas weighing 260 grains (16.85 gm) each. On the coin of Vima the king stands in profile, turned left. His right hand is held over a small fire altar and is making some offerings. His features are realistically depicted, as a corpulent figure with a long heavy face and a large nose. He is wearing a Kushana cloak, tall Gilgit boots and a conical hat on the head with streamers. A large club with knobbed handle or a mace can be seen in the field to the right. A trident battle-axe appears on the left. His monogram is placed on the right. The legend in Greek letters is not legible. A clear inscription reads thus: *Basileus Basileon Soter Megas Ooemo Kadphises* (the king of kings, the great saviour Vima Kadphises).

On the reverse, god Siva stands frontally and leans against *Nandi* (the bull) with his left hand resting on its hump while he is holding a trident in his right hand. A symbol of *Nandipada* usually placed in the left upper field is not clear. A circular Kharoshti legend though not very legible is given around the edge: *Maharajasa rajadhirajasa sarvaloga Iswarasa Maheswarasa Vima Kathaphisasa Tradara* (the great king, king of kings, lord of the world, devotee of Maheswara Vima Kadphises, the defender).

On Huvishka's copper pana (Fig. 4.2) helmeted king is presented lounging on a low couch or bench. While his left elbow is resting on a cushion, the right hand is resting on the waist; and the right foot is on the bench. This is an informal presentation of the king; yet a 'halo' around the king's head is shown as a reminder of the greatness of the king. The legend on the right in Greek letters is not clear. On the other side, a standing god facing left in profile is depicted. He wears a cap and a radiating cloud around his head is shown. His extended right hand holds a garland, while his left hand is resting at the waist. He is wearing a long sword, hanging down. On the beaded border a blurred legend in Greek letters, MIIRO (the sun god), appears on the right. A monogram is shown in the left field.

With the remarkable increase in trade, the exchange of ideas between the East and the West was also significant during the Kushana rule. Indian pilgrims travelling the 'silk road' introduced Buddhism to China in the early centuries of AD. Missionaries of the Great Yueh-Chih played an important role in the propagation of this religion. The Kushanas were great patrons of Buddhism. On the counsel of Ashavaghosa, Kanishka convened the *Fourth Great Buddhist Council* in Kashmir that marked the beginning of Mahayana Buddhism. At this conference authorised commentaries on Buddhist canon were prepared, and engraved on copper plates; the spread of Indian culture as far as the borders of China probably resulted from Kushanas' influence.

Fusion of eastern and western art that began with the Greeks, was reinforced during the reign of the Kushanas. While Buddha was being shaped in Graeco-Roman fashion in Gandhara, the native Mathura School portrayed him in the Indian 'Yaksha' tradition. While encouraging these two schools, the Kushanas also gave equal patronage to their own imperial art of Iranian derivation. Its style of portrayal is realistic, with emphasis on power and wealth. Their commitment to Buddhist art can be seen in the world's largest Buddha figures, 175 feet and 120 feet tall, that were carved into a cliff at Bamian in the central mountains of Afghanistan during the 3rd and 4th centuries AD.

The story of the Kushanas is a great example to cite the possibilities of transformation of the war-like belligerence of man into a saint-like serenity. And certainly they had demonstrated how a commitment to one's own beliefs calls for an understanding of others' rights to their individual beliefs; and hence the need for universal tolerance and syncretism for peaceful co-existence of human race.

Fig. 5.1 Coins of Srimukha Sata, Gauthamiputra Sathakarni, Vashistiputra Pulumavi. 2nd Century B.C. to 2nd Century A.D.
Obverse: With the legends *Srimukasata, Siri Satakanisa, Siri Pulumavisa.*

5. THE SATHAVAHANAS*

Andhras were first mentioned in the ancient Aitareya Brahmana. They were also mentioned thrice in Mahabharata, but on each occasion in conjunction with different peoples. Pliny the elder, a Roman historian, refers to Andhras in his "Natural History" thus: "...there is an island in the Ganges of great extent, inhabited by a single tribe called Modogalinga (Three Kalinga)...but a still more

*Courtesy: The Hindu. This article was published by the author under the title 'Reminders of a great dynasty' in The Hindu dated 10-1-1993.

Fig. 5.2 Coins of Srimukha Sata, Gauthamiputra Sathakarni, Vashistiputra Pulumavi. *Reverse:* With Ujjain symbol.

powerful people are the Andarae who have many villages, thirty fortified and walled towns and their king has a standing army of 1,00,000 infantry, 2,000 cavalry and 1000 elephants." From these statements we may infer that the valley of Ganges from the frontier of Magadha to sea was possessed in the third century BC by Kalingae and Andarae. In the Peutingerian tables Andhras were mentioned as Andre-Indi. Thus, most of the western geographers assigned a northern habitat to Andhras.

An Asoka's edict, the 16th tablet at Shahbazgarhi, lists contemporary potentates. Beginning with five Greek kings it ends with Andhras and Pulindas recognizing Andhras as a substantive power during the reign of Asoka between 269 to 232 BC. Asoka sent Buddhist missionaries to Andhra to propagate the idea and practice of Dhamma (Dharma). It is presumed by modern writers that the Andhra kingdom came into existence after the death of Asoka in 232 BC, when Simuka (Srimukha) asserted his complete independence from the Mauryan empire.

Inscriptions found in caves such as those at Nanaghat, Nasik, Karli and Kanheri commemorate the early rulers, Srimukha, his brother Krishna, and his son Sathakarni or Sathavahana I. From these inscriptions we come to know that they belong to the Andhra tribe and their family name was Sathavahana. Our ancient books, Matsya Purana, Vayu Purana, Vishnu Purana and Bhagavatha, provide us with lists of the Andhra kings and their years of reign. But modern scholars do not agree with the chronological order as given in the Puranas. The first 21 kings of the Puranic lists are unknown to numismatic series, that is, coins struck by them were not yet found. There are some coins of nine kings of the Puranic list, indicating that these rulers were of considerable importance. Besides, there is evidence of coins of a few rulers, who were not mentioned in either Puranas, or inscriptions. These coins suggest that there were several other rulers, such as Siva Sathakarni, Sri Chandra Sati, Rudra Sathakarni, Kumbha Sathakarni and Krishnakarni.

The Sathavahana kingdom came into prominence with the fall of the Sunga and Kanva rulers of Vidisha in 27 BC; and the kingdom was gradually expanded to western and southern India. Sathakarni or Sathavahana I (AD 106–130) ruled with two more capitals, Banavasi (Vaijayanthi) in the west and Prathisthanapura (modern Paithan) in the north, on the banks of the Godavari. The proximity of western Ksatrapas in Western India gave rise to intermittent wars between them. Ksatrapa Nahapana initially penetrated as far south as Nasik. These territories were again regained by Sathavahana I. His conquests ranged over vast expanses of land stretching approximately from Rajasthan in the North-West to Andhra in the South-East and Gujarat in the West and Kalinga in the East, extending to the entire Southern India. As it was the first empire in the south, he was called Dakshinapathapathi (Lord of the South), Sathakarni's son Vashistiputra Pulumavi (130–159 AD) was married to the daughter of Ksatrapa Rudradaman but it did not result in the expected peace with Ksatrapas. He expanded the empire to the east and to the north-east. His inscriptions and coins were found all over the empire. Siva Sathakarni (AD 159–166) is known from coins found in Krishna and Godavari districts. The distribution area of Yajna Sathakarni's (AD 174–203) regional coins is spread over the Krishna-Godavari districts, the Chanda district of Maharashtra, Berar, Western Konkan and Saurashtra.

The local character of later numismatic issues and their distribution pattern indicated the subsequent fragmentation of the Sathavahana empire. The Maharathis, the feudatories of Andhras, who originally issued local coins with their title "Maharathisa" had started issuing coins mentioning their names also, thus indicating their independence (Fig. 5.4, 5.5). Different areas in the Western Deccan experienced the emergence of new local powers such as the Cutus, Abhiras and Kuras. The Vakatakas started asserting themselves in Berar region. By the third century AD the Sathavahana empire broke into small pockets of control among the family members.

The Nanaghat inscription of queen Naganika, wife of Sathakarni, and the Kanheri inscription of Yajna Sathakarni throw some light on the coinage in circulation. Sums of money were estimated in Karsapanas, undoubtedly of silver, which were in circulation in both regions. Silver coins of Nahapana restruck by Gauthamiputra Sathakarni were Karsapanas. So also were the silver coins of Yajna Sathakarni of Saurashtra fabric. A hoard containing 7,668 coins of this type was found some time ago at Amaravathi, (Guntur dist. A.P.). These silver coins weigh 34 to 36 grains (2.2 to 2.3 gm) unlike the Karsapanas of the Mauryan period which weigh 57 to 58 grains (3.69 to 3.75 gm). This type of silver coins were used by the contemporary Ksatrapas and later by the Abhiras in Nasik district and Trikutakas in Gujarat and Saurashtra. This weight standard is supposed to be that of hemi-drachms of the Graeco-Indian princes. One of the inscriptions at Nasik narrates the rate of exchange between karsapana and Suvarna (the standard gold coin) as 1 to 35. Since the gold coins of Sathavahanas are not yet reported, we presume that the Suvarnas referred here are those issued by the Kushanas. If we take the weight of Karsapana as 36 grains and that of Suvarna as 124 grains, we find that the ratio of silver to gold at that time was 1 to 10.

The coins of the Andhra monetary system differ from those of the rest of Southern India, having a special character of their own. Use of lead predominates in Andhra coinage throughout the empire; while there were also a few silver, copper and potin issues (Fig. 5.1, 5.2, 5.3). The Andhra coins are stamped with

Fig. 5.3 Potin and lead coins of Sathavahana period with Ujjain symbol. 2nd Century B.C. to 2nd Century A.D.

Fig. 5.4 Lead coins of the Maharathis, the feudatories of Sathavahanas.
Obverse: An elephant facing left with Brahmi legends *Maharathisa* and *Maharathisa Sivakhadasa*. 2nd Century A.D.

Fig. 5.5 Lead coins of the Maharathis, the feudatories of Sathavahanas.
Reverse: A Buddhist tree in railing. 2nd Century A.D.

Buddhist characters. The obverse has a figure of a lion or a horse or an elephant with the name of the sovereign, and some later coins carry the effigy of the king. Often the reverse has the Buddhist cross or wheel, often called Ujjain symbol. Sometimes a tree-in-railing is seen on the reverse, symbolising the sacred tree under which Buddha was enlightened. These coins vary greatly in size. They are generally round and sometimes square. Some were struck only on one side, the reverse being plain.

The later Sathavahanas were the first among the Indian sovereigns to circulate silver currency with the royal bust on it. They were designed after the silver issues of Ksatrapa Nahapana. Over two hundred such coins were reported at ancient sites on the bank of the Narmada, Godavari, Krishna and in the upper Mahanadi valley. These are attributed to Gauthamiputra Sathakarni, Vashistiputra Pulumavi, Gauthamiputra Yajna Sathakarni and Vijaya Sathakarni. In these portrait series the king's profile is to the right with prominent nose and thick lips; and the earlobe is hanging with a loop with suspended *Karanakundala*. He is also seen wearing a crest jewel. The king's name is given on the obverse in Brahmi characters. On the reverse a six-arched hill and a part of the Ujjain symbol are seen. The legend on the reverse is in some Dravidian script. These were the bilingual issues, the first ever to appear on South Indian coins.

Recently, for the first time, portrait coins of lead issued by Sathavahanas were discovered in the excavations at Adam (Kuhi taluq, Nagpur dist.) in the Vidarbha region. Such coins were also reported from the Wainganga river basin. These lead coins resembling their silver patterns were produced by the die-striking technique. Obverse and reverse are identical with those of silver portrait issues. Two coins are attributed to Vashistiputra Pulumavi and one to Gauthamiputra Yajna Sathakarni.

Nine coins of Sathavahana period are shown here: seven of them having the Ujjain symbols on the reverse are the Sathavahana issues. Three are made of lead, on the obverse of which can be seen a crude depiction of an animal. It is not clear whether it is a horse or an elephant. And three are made of potin, an alloy of copper and silver. The square coin made of copper is rare and is produced by the die-striking process.

The other two large lead coins are Maharathisa issues. On their obverse an elephant facing left is clear while on the reverse a tree-in-railing is depicted. The legends are written in Brahmi characters. On one coin, the legend "Maharathisa" is written; this probably was issued when Maharathis were feudatories of Sathavahanas. The other coin has a legend "Maharathisa Sivakhadasa"; and must have been issued after asserting their independence from Sathavahanas.

It was under the Sathavahanas that the historic period proper began in Andhra Desa. Although there was no clear indication as to whether the central administrative system was evolved, an extensive system of currency was introduced throughout the empire.

The material prosperity of Andhras is reflected in their liberal patronage of Buddhist and Brahminical communities, as enumerated in the contemporary inscriptions at Nanaghat and Nasik. Andhras were also great builders, their principal city Amaravathi contained Buddhist monuments inaugurating a new style of architecture and narrative sculpture. The Amaravathi style is also seen in the stupa remains at Jaggayyapeta, Nagarjunakonda and Goli in Andhra Pradesh. This style spread to Sri Lanka as in Anuradhapura, and to much of South-East Asia.

Fig. 6.1 Silver Karsapanas of Saka Ksatrapas Vijayasena, Damajada Sri III, Rudrasena II, Bhartradaman, Viswasena and Rudra Simha II, Western India A.D. 115–388.

6. THE WESTERN KSATRAPAS

A novel form of government ruled by independent governors, originally a Persian innovation, was introduced for the first time in India by Achaemenid kings when they occupied Punjab and Indus regions as early as sixth century B.C. In Persia the governor of a province is called *Kshathrapavan* (the protector of land). This term was Hellenized into *Satrap* and its Sanskrit equivalent is *Ksatrapa*. In India, as in Persia, Ksatrapas were viceroys technically appointed by a sovereign; but later they became hereditary sub-kings. This in turn elevated the position of the sovereign as king of kings.

In India there was another higher rank of Mahaksatrapa (the great satrap), who occupied a position of greater power than a Ksatrapa who is yet to prove his mettle to deserve this position. Occasionally it was also won directly by personal achievement. He frequently issued inscriptions in whatever era he chose to follow and minted his own coins, but he still accepted the suzerainty of the king of kings.

There were at least four clearly ascertained centres of Satrapal governments in ancient India. A Ksatrapa of Kapisa, who ruled the province after Saka conquest, is known from an inscription on Mainkyala Cylinder. That Taxila was ruled by a Ksatrapa dynasty is clear from a copper plate inscription of Patika son of Ksatrapa Liaka Kusuluka, dated in the 78th year of Moga (Maues). Northern Ksatrapas of Mathura are known from the coins of Mahaksatrapa Rajuvala and Ksatrapa Sodasa and their inscriptions on the lion-capital. A Saranath inscription dated in the 3rd year of Kaniska shows that at a later date a Mahaksatrapa Khara Pallana and a Ksatrapa Vanaspara were paying allegiance to Kushana king Kaniska. The Ksatrapas of Malwa and Saurashtra stood prominent in the West as is evident from their extensive coinage and inscriptions. They ruled for two and a half centuries from about 119 to 388 AD.

The Western Ksatrapas hailed from two distinct families. The first was that of Ksatrapas represented by Bhumaka and Nahapana who established their rule in Western Ghats. The second royal house was that of Castana whose capital according to Ptolemy was Ujjain in West Malwa. He was a contemporary of Andhra King Vashistiputra Pulumavi. It seems to be certain that the name Nahapana is Persian in origin and that the name Ghsamotika father of Castana is Scythic (Saka). Whatever be their lineage, the later Ksatrapas were known as Sakas as is evident from their inscriptions. In the Allahabad inscription of Samudra Gupta the Sakas who were mentioned together with Daivaputra Shahi Shahanu Shahis may reasonably supposed to be Western Ksatrapas. That they belonged to different families is certain; but their use of Kharoshti alphabet, character of their names and titles suggest that they were of northern origin, and viceroys of a northern power, probably that of Kushanas. In most of the inscriptions the Pahlava Ksatrapas were mentioned as Ksaharatas while the Saka Ksatrapas were called Karddamakas.

Bhumaka the earliest ruler of Ksaharata Family is known only by his copper coins found in the coastal regions of Gujarat, Kathiawar and Malwa. An arrow, a disc and a thunderbolt appear on the obverse of his coins; while a lion-capital and Dharmachakra, the wheel of law of Buddhist faith, are depicted on the reverse. His name in Sanskrit is given on the obverse in Brahmi script as *Ksaharata Ksatrapasa Bhumakasa* and on the reverse it is rendered in Prakrit using Kharoshti letters.

Bhumaka was succeeded by Nahapana. His kingdom included South Gujarat, North Konkan from Broach to Sopara, Nasik and Poona districts, Saurashtra (Kathiawar), Kukura (probably some part of Rajasthan), Akara (East Malwa), Avanthi (West Malwa) and Pushkara in Ajmer. The later rulers extended their dominions till they embraced all the flourishing ports on the West Coast with their valuable sea-borne trade.

Nahapana was the first among the Western Ksatrapas to have placed his portrait on the obverse of his silver coins; he, however, retained his dynastic symbols—arrow, disc and thunderbolt, on the reverse. His silver coinage is similar in size, weight and fabric to that of hemi-drachms of the Graeco-Indian Princes Apollodotus and Menander which were in circulation previously in the Western region. His coin legends are triolingual. The obverse is in Graeco-Roman letters, which in fact is the transliteration of the reverse Sanskrit legend *Rajno Ksaharatasa Nahapanasa* (The king Ksaharata Nahapana). Similar legend in Prakrit is also given on the reverse in Kharoshti script. His titles 'Ksatrapa' and 'Mahaksatrapa' do not occur in his coin legends, though they appear in his inscriptions issued during 41th and 46th years of Saka era (119 and 124 AD). Unlike Ksatrapa Bhumaka, Nahapana was always called a Rajah.

Castana, a Saka Ksatrapa, took over after Nahapana. He struck silver Karsapanas both as Ksatrapa and Mahaksatrapa, which are similar to those of

Nahapana with royal bust on the obverse and tri-lingual legends. While he was a Ksatrapa he issued two varieties of silver coins, distinguished by different reverse types. In the first variety the symbols of a crescent and a star, probably of Parthian origin, are depicted, whereas in the second type there was an addition of a chaitya (a three-arched hill). And soon the new motif took a predominant position at the centre, while crescent and star are reduced to a subordinate position of mere symbols. This type was continued even after Castana assumed the title of Mahaksatrapa. It later became the dynastic emblem for the succeeding 26 rulers of this line, who issued the same type of silver coinage for more than two and a half centuries.

Jivadaman, the fifth Ksatrapa who ruled about AD 178, was the first Indian king ever to have added the year of issue to the inscriptions on his coins. The year mentioned was in Saka era, a system of dating that began in 78 A.D. It is said to have been initiated by Kaniska, who assumed the title Shao Nano Shao (King of Kings). The Western Ksatrapas who appear to have accepted his suzerainty adopted this era, and used it in their inscriptions and coinage. From the time of Jivadaman onwards all the Ksatrapas regularly recorded the year of issue on their coins. These are of greatest historical significance and service in helping to date events here and elsewhere in India down to the year 395 AD when the Guptas conquered their territories.

Sanskrit legends on coins during the time of Castana and Nahapana were undoubtedly in Greek script with an admixture of Roman characters; but later the form of the letters deteriorated to such an extent that their meaning seems to have been lost entirely. Though they continued to be present on the obverse they looked more like ornamental flourishes than legends. On the later coinage the Kharoshti letters disappeared, but the Sanskrit legends in Brahmi characters were continued (Fig. 6.1).

A special feature of these legends is the presence of a patronymic. While their Andhra contemporaries used metronymics, these rulers identified themselves with their fathers in such legends as *Rajno Ksatrapasa Ghsamotikaputra Castana* (The King Ksatrapa Castana, son of Ghsamotika). As every ruler recorded the name of his father in these legends it is possible to trace the ruling line with precision; and it is known that each successor up to Viswasena (304 A.D.) was the son of a prince who ruled as Ksatrapa or Mahaksatrapa. But the family of Rudra Simha II who succeeded in 305 AD is an exception. Though it is almost certain that he is closely connected with the main line, his father Swami Jivadaman did not bear any princely title.

Another feature revealed by the coin legends is that the names of the family of Castana are Indianized immediately—his son is named Jayadaman. And they

Fig. 6.2 A silver Karsapana of Vijayasena (obverse) with the portrait of the king with corrupt Greek inscription. 240–250 A.D.

Fig. 6.3 A silver Karsapana of Vijayasena (reverse) with a Sanskrit legend *Rajno Mahaksatrapasa Damasena Putrasa Rajnah Ksatrapasa Vijaya senasa*. 240–250 A.D.

remain throughout the same in character always ending in daman, simha, and sena, with a single exception of Damajada.

The denominations and weight standards of potin, copper and lead coins of the Western Ksatrapas are doubtful, but their silver coins are undoubtedly called Karsapanas in their inscriptions. They weighed only 34 to 36 grains unlike the Karsapana of Mauryan period which weighed 57.6 grains (32 ratis). A Nasik inscription of Rishabhadatta (Usavadatta), a 'Saka' viceroy and son-in-law of Nahapana, contains important information that the rate of exchange between a Karsapana and Suvarna was 1 to 35. No gold coins were issued by the Western Ksatrapas. The Suvarna here may be presumed to be the denari (124 grains) of Kushanas, which might have been in circulation. It can be deduced that the ratio of silver to gold at that time was approximately 1 to 10.

Rishabhadatta's inscription, which recorded his endowments to the monks residing in Trirashmi mountains in Govardhana in Nasik district, throws some light on the interest rates prevailing at that time as well as the type of investments available. Among these endowments, one investment of 2000 Karsapanas with a guild of weavers at Govardhana bears interest at the rate of 1 per cent per mensem (Vadhi Padika Sata), and the amount thus forthcoming annually, that is 240 Karsapanas, was provided for the monks living in the cave during rainy season with 12 Karsapanas each for clothing. Another investment with a guild of weavers at Govardhana is of 1000 Karsapanas at 3/4 per cent interest per mensem (Vadhi Payuna Padika Sata) and the annual interest from this source, that is 90 Karsapanas, was provided for the monks with Kushanamula. The meaning of this term is doubtful. One scholar translates this as "money for outside life", and according to another scholar the reference here is made to the custom of Kathina—the privilege of wearing extra robes, which was granted to the monks during the rainy season.

Silver Karsapanas of Vijayasena, Damajada Sri III, Rudra Sena II, Bhartrdaman, Viswasena and Rudra Simha II are shown in the picture (Fig. 6.1). A coin of Ksatrapa Vijaya Sena issued in the year 160 of Saka era (238 AD) has been shown separately (Fig. 6.2, 6.3). His portrait facing right is on the obverse with fragmentary letters of Greek origin around the edge. The date of issue in Brahmi numerals, generally placed behind the head, is out of flan here. A beautiful Sanskrit inscription in Brahmi characters is on the reverse. Only part of it is visible: *"ma senasa putrasa Rajnah Vija"*. On similar coins, the full inscription, as shown here, reads thus: *Rajno Mahaksatrapasa Dama Senasa Putrasa Rajnah Ksatrapasa Vijaya Senasa* (The king Ksatrapa Vijaya Sena son of the great king Mahaksatrapa Dama Sena). A three-arched-chaitya is depicted at the centre, with a crescent and star above and a line below.

On observing the clarity and neatness of the fabric of these coins, one scholar remarks that they look as if the race to whom they belong was by no means backward in civilisation and commerce; and it is notable that the land of Gujarat is that which would be natural entrepot of trade between marts of India on the one hand and those of Rome and Egypt on the other.

That maritime trade had flourished in Western India during Ksatrapa rule is fully authenticated in Periplus Maris Erythraei written in 1st century AD as it lists a series of ports along the Indian coasts, which included Broach (Bharuch or Bharuckaccha) and Sopara (Surparaka). Ancient Hebrew books refer to Indian Port of Ophir, which is identified as Surparaka of west coast, described as a market for gold, spices, precious stones, ivory, apes and peacocks. Other Indian exports included teak, cedar, pepper, pearls, silk and textiles. The strong tradition of enterprise and trade initiated by these Saka rulers had such a great impact that even today the Western region, Gujarat in particular, stands out to be the torch bearer for all the Indian enterprises.

7. THE GOLDEN AGE OF THE GUPTAS*

The origin of the Guptas is obscure, all one knows is that they hailed from eastern Uttar Pradesh and that Sri Gupta and Ghatotkacha were the first two kings. The third, Chandra Gupta took the title of Maharajadhiraja (king of kings) and with his marriage to a Lichchavi princess added Magadha to his empire, enhancing the power and prestige of the new kingdom. This event was celebrated in a series of gold coins.

According to a long Prashasti (eulogy) inscribed on a pillar in Prayaga (Allahabad), Chandra Gupta held an assembly of counsellors and members of the royal family in 330 A.D., at which he formally nominated his son Samudra Gupta to succeed him. The coins of an obscure king, Kacha Gupta, suggest that there may have been other contenders to the throne. Samudra Gupta proved to be a strategic genius. The military prowess of his army was so invincible that he extended his empire to the base of the Himalayas in the north to the Brahmaputra river in the east, to the banks of Narmada river in the south, and to the river Jamuna and the Chambal valley in the west. He celebrated the Ashvamedha (horse-sacrifice) reviving the Vedic ritual, probably at the conclusion of his campaigns, and also celebrated the event by issuing gold coins.

He was succeeded by his son Chandra Gupta II in A.D. 375, though there is some evidence that there had been an intermediate ruler. His major campaigns were against Saka rulers of Ujjain, success of which was celebrated in a series of silver coins.

He was succeeded by Kumara Gupta who ruled for 42 years (413–455 A.D.). During the reign of his son, Skanda Gupta, the empire faced the threat of the invading Huns. There was a gradual decline of the empire during the last Guptas—Buddha Gupta, Chandra Gupta III, Prakashaditya, Vinaya Gupta, Narasimha Gupta, Kumara Gupta III and Vishnu Gupta. By A.D. 543 the Gupta kingdom went into oblivion.

---

*Courtesy: The Hindu. This article was published by the author under the title 'Reminders of a golden regime' in The Hindu dated 17-3-1991.

Fig. 7.1 A gold coin of Chandragupta Vikramaditya. 375–413 A.D.
Obverse: The king standing left, holding a bow in left hand and an arrow in the right hand. Garuda standard on the left. *Chandra* below the left arm. Legend: *Devasri Maharajadhiraja Sri Chandragupta.*

The splendid gold coinage of the Guptas with its various types and varieties and its inscriptions in Sanskrit, now appearing for the first time, are the finest examples of pure Indian art (Fig. 7.1, 7.2, 7.3). That it rained gold during the Gupta reign sounds a poetic exaggeration, and yet it was a fact that there was such an abundance of gold received as tribute that Samudra Gupta struck coins only in the yellow metal.

The earlier issues of Gupta coinage followed the Kushana model closely in design and execution, and yet they displayed originality and superior workmanship, modelling the king's features with careful attention to detail. The king still wears a Kushana dress, and the Kushana symbol appears on the reverse. In place of Siva's trident is a Garuda-headed standard. In the later issues the Kushana trousers are replaced by the Indian *dhoti*, and the cap is shortened. The king holds a spear or battle-axe or a sword, instead of a trident. In spite of all these modifications the Gupta coinage retained the method of placing the name of the king perpendicularly under the left hand, Chinese fashion. Probably these coins were issued for circulation in the territories formerly ruled by the Kushanas.

On the reverse, the seated goddess Ardhoksho resembles Lakshmi. Instead of the name of the goddess, the king's name appears in Brahmi characters. On the earlier coins she continues to hold pasa (fillet) in the left hand and a cornucopia in the right. On the latter coins she holds a lotus in the right hand.

The most common Gupta coin is that which shows the king holding a bow in his left hand. This type was issued by almost all the rulers of the dynasty. Here the king also holds an arrow in the right hand. But there were several varieties of this type issued by Chandra Gupta II and Kumara Gupta, showing the king facing the left or right, wearing a dress or bare-bodied, with some variations in the depictions. On the coins of Samudra Gupta and Chandra Gupta II, the king is holding a spear or sword. On those of Kacha Gupta he is holding a standard surmounted by the Chakra (Chakradwaja). On Kumara Gupta's coins, he is holding a sword or battle-axe instead of the standard, and sometimes a small dwarf is shown below the right hand.

The Gupta mints had issued 16 other types, quite artistic in their appearance and original in content. In one, the king and queen are portrayed standing face to face. Such coins were issued by Chandra Gupta I, Kumara Gupta I and Skanda Gupta, on the reverse is the family name of the queen "Lichchavaya". This relationship is a matter of pride to the king. It is so original that scholars do not believe they were issued by the first emperor of this dynasty, though they bear the names of Chandra Gupta and Kumara Devi. They are believed to have been issued by Samudra Gupta as commemorative coins. The coins issued by Kumara Gupta I and Skanda Gupta have no names of the king and queen.

Fig. 7.2 A gold coin of Chandragupta Vikramaditya. 375–413 A.D.
Reverse: Goddess Lakshmi seated on a lotus holding a lotus in the left hand and a noose in the right. Legend: In Sanskrit *Srivikrama*.

Fig. 7.3 Gold coins of Gupta period (electroplated reproductions). 320–480 A.D.

The inscriptions on the Gupta coins are equally interesting as the designs on them. The obverse legend which encircles the design is usually in the form of a verse in *Upagiti* or some other Sanskrit metre. Some of them praise the glory of the king on earth and his future bliss in heaven, attained through good deeds and sacrifices. For example, a coin of Chandra Gupta II says, *Vikramaditya Prithvim Avitha Divam Jayatha* (Vikramaditya having conquered the earth wins heaven by good works). And there are more ornate legends on horseman-type coins of Kumara Gupta, *Gupta Kula Vyoma Sasi Jayatya Jayojita Mahendra* (The unconquered Mahendra, the invincible, the moon in the sky of Gupta line, is victorious).

When a verse appears on the obverse, there appears on the reverse a distinct legend with the king's title. Finally, on the obverse of almost all coins, a part of the king's name appears vertically under or near the king's left arm as Samudra or Chandra or Kumara in Brahmi characters. This method of writing from top to bottom may be traced back through the later Kushana coins to a Chinese source.

No silver coins were issued by the earlier Guptas. For the first time, they were issued by Vikramaditya Chandra Gupta and resemble the pattern of the Ksatrapa coins. The symbol "three-arched hill" is replaced by "Garuda", the royal emblem of the Guptas. Their circulation was confined to the western region.

The Guptas rarely issued copper coins. Eight varieties are known. The obverse followed the pattern of gold and silver issues. On the reverse the royal seal of "Garuda with the wings spread" at the top is depicted with the king's title below. Most of these coins were attributed to Chandra Gupta II and Kumara Gupta.

The picture here shows one archer-type coin issued by Vikramaditya Chandra Gupta. On the obverse, the king is standing, with the Garuda standard to the left and the bow to the right. The inscription in Nagari characters is written around the flan. Some of the letters are not legible. Under the left arm the word "Chandra" written vertically in Brahmi characters is very clear. On the reverse a seated goddess is portrayed, holding a lotus in the left hand and a pasa (fillet) in the right. A legend, Sri Vikramah, written at the edge of right flan in Brahmi letters, is quite clear. This was the standard gold coin called Suvarna weighing 124 grains (7.8 gm).

Marked by the most flourishing artistic activities, the age of the Guptas remains the most golden in India's history.

Fig. 8.1 Pallava coins (obverse) with lion and nandi symbols. 6th Century A.D.

8. PALLAVA HERITAGE*

Scholars believe that the early Pallavas were a pastoral race akin to the hardy, warlike Kurumbas settled in eastern parts of ancient Kunthala. Yet some others trace their origin to the Parthian invaders. In the Vishnu Purana 'Pallavas' and 'Pahlavas' are given as variants of 'Pahnavas'. The Pahlavas or Parthavas are referred to along with Sakas and Yavanas (the Scythians and the Greeks) and Kambhojas and Gandharas in the epics, Ramayana and Mahabharatha, and Manu's Dharmasastra.

Pahlava princes like Vonones, Spalahores and Spalarises had initially settled in small kingdoms in the North, but in the later centuries their descendants survived as chieftains and feudatories. From a Girnar (Junagadh) inscription, we come to know that during the reign of Asoka, his viceroy Tushaspa, a Yavana with a Persian name, provided conduits for Sudarsana lake, and that Suvishaka, a Pahlava viceroy of Rudradaman, repaired it in the second century A.D. In another Nasik inscription of the same period, Gauthami Balasri, mother of Sathakarni, proudly mentions her grandson Pulumavi as the destroyer of the Sakas, Yavanas and Pallavas. Thus, one can conclude that the Pallavas were settled in the territories of the Andhra Sathavahanas and the Western Ksatrapas, as governors or viceroys. They came to power after the fall of the Andhras, and by the fourth century A.D. they were established in southern India with three capitals. They stood prominent in the East in the land between the Krishna and the Godavari, the original country of the Sathavahanas, with their capital at Vengi. Their rule extended to Nellore in the South and Bellary in the West. Many copper-plate grants (Tamra Sasanams) that came to light provide one with lists of numerous kings: Kanagopa, Chuta Pallava, Vira Kurucha, Skanda Shishya, Kumara Krishna, Buddha Varma and so on.

The Pallavas of Kanchipuram rose to power towards the end of the sixth century A.D. In their copper-plate grants, the first ever in Tamil, the early kings often mention places just to the north in Andhra Desa suggesting that they had

*Courtesy: The Hindu. This article was published by the author under the title 'Pallava heritage' in The Hindu dated 31-3-1991.

migrated to the Kanchipuram area (Thondamandalam). Those of later kings indicate that they became dominant after defeating Achyuta Vikrantra of the Kalabhara dynasty who ruled over the Tamil country.

The maritime trade and commercial enterprise of the Pallavas are amply attested by the ancient Chinese, Persian and Roman coins found at seaports like Mamallapuram on the Coromandal coast.

The earliest coins of the Pallavas, a legacy from the Sathavahanas, are indistinguishable from those of the Kurumbas with the symbol of an animal like the horse on the obverse, but there was a gradual development in their form and fabric. Gold and copper dominate their coinage while there were a few issues in silver. While all of them are thick and dumpy in fabric, the gold issues are relatively thin. The denominations are not clear, but the copper coins of different weights suggest that there are at least two denominations of copper fanams. Most of the issues are cast and die struck, and well executed. Some of the specimens are as good as those of the nineteenth century mints.

On most of the coins a "maned lion" appears on the obverse. This royal emblem is seen on most of the Pallava copper-plate grants, and on the walls of the temples built under royal patronage. Nandi, the sacred bull, a revered symbol of Saivism is also displayed occasionally on some issues, probably commemorating such important events as the conversion of Mahendravarman from Jainism. Sometimes a two-masted ship, such as the one seen on some Sathavahana issues, is also depicted, indicating the sea-faring interests of the Pallavas.

Generally only one symbol, perhaps of religious significance, is seen on the reverse, though there are several varieties: a swastika, a wheel, a bow, a fish, an umbrella, a horse, a lion or a sacred vase. Buddhist and Jaina emblems appear on the coins of the earlier period, while the Saiva and Vaishnava symbols emerged on the later issues in tune with the changing religious patronage of the kings.

No other information is available on most of the coins except a short legend which sounds more like a title than the name of a king. Mahendravarman I is known by many titles: "Guna Bhara" (a king blessed with noble qualities), "Sri Bhara" (king endowed with great wealth); Narasimha Varman I thrived on several titles such as "Mahamalla"—a great warrior, "Chaityakari"—a builder of temples, "Vatapikondan"—the conqueror of Vatapi (Badami); Narasimha Varman II is often referred to as "Raja Simha"—lion among kings and "Sri Nidhi"—a king who is a treasuretrove. From these titles it is possible to attribute a coin to a particular king. But in most cases they remain undecipherable as the titles, such as "Manapara", do not reveal the identity of the king.

Fig. 8.2 Pallava coins (reverse) with a vase-like symbol. 6th Century A.D.

Here are seen four coins of the early Pallava period (Fig. 8.1, 8.2), all of them are in copper and silver; and in all, the obverse is fully covered by copper while the reverse shows silver at the centre and copper at the edge. Without exception the silver portion is struck with an emblem of some religious significance. To achieve this special effect, it appears that the old silver coins, probably belonging to the previous regimes, were first put in the moulds in such a way that the emblem appears on the reverse, the casting is completed by pouring the molten copper on it and then impressing with an obverse die. One of them is larger in size, 19 mm wide weighing 7.72 grains (5 gm). The rest are small, 15 mm in width and 15.14 grains (3.33 gm) by weight each. The obverse is fully covered by copper. A maned lion can be seen on three of them. The lion faces right with its right paw raised, depicting a roaring gesture, and its mouth wide open, exposing its teeth. A short sword can be seen in front of the lion. There is one small coin (extreme right), probably a commemorative issue having a decorated Nandi, a sacred bull. On the obverse of all, the space between the emblem and the edge is filled with dots or radiating lines.

The reverse in all the cases is similar, having a clearly visible centre of silver, on which a sacred vase or standard is depicted. It is positioned between two tall trifid lamp stands or standards, the entire emblem is enclosed in a broad circle of radiating lines.

A legend in a Southern form of Brahmi characters is clearly visible on a small coin (extreme left), just above the lion. The letters "Sri Bha Ra" are legible. There seem to be two more letters which are illegible. This particular coin may safely be attributed to Mahendravarman I. The remaining three are, no doubt, Pallava issues, but in the absence of any legend it is not possible to attribute them to any particular king.

The Pallavas supported Buddhism and Jainism initially, but they later patronised Puranic faith and built temples devoted to Siva and Vishnu. In the earlier phase (610–690 A.D.) their focus was on monolithic temples each carved out of a single boulder-like granite rock such as the five chariots (pandava rathas) at Mamallapuram; it includes sculptured rock relief monuments and cave temples popularly known as "Arjuna's Penance", "Descent of Ganga" and "Varaha caves", and the rock-cut cave temples at Tiruchirapalli and Kunnandar Koil.

The glorious second phase (690–900 A.D.) paved the way for a unique Dravidian style, a forerunner to all the styles of South Indian temple-architecture. Many of the 126 present-day temples at Kanchipuram trace their origin to the

Pallavas. The influence of this style spread to all parts of India and South-East-Asia as well; it is clearly visible in the pyramid-like structures of the great temples at Angkor Wat (Cambodia), Borobudur (Java) and Puradesa Pasban (Bali, Indonesia).

The most decorous jewellery and attire known from the carved figures in cave temples, bronze sculptures, and those adorned by characters in epics and dramas provide one an index to the prosperity and progress achieved by the Pallavas. The remarkable role played by them in the cultural advancement of medieval southern India has no parallel. It is strange that a devout people, brave and adventurous, who enjoyed a high degree of civilisation have become so merged in the population and are now remembered only by their coins and inscriptions, copper-plates and monoliths.

Fig. 9.2 Copper coins of Vijayanagara (obverse) with the Garuda symbol. 1336–1614 A.D.

9. GLORY THAT WAS VIJAYANAGARA

The great forgotten city of Vijayanagara and its empire were founded by two brothers Harihara and Bukka in 1336 AD to serve mainly as a strong bulwark against the inroads of the hostile Muslim invaders from the North. Extending over an area of 23 square kilometres, it was strategically located in an easily defensible position on the southern banks of Tungabhadra river. Ruins of the city are partly occupied by the modern village Hampi, Bellary district, Karnataka. Initially, it was called Hosapattana, the new city and later Hasthinavathi, perhaps the

Fig. 9.3 Copper coins of Vijayanagara (reverse) with Nagari legend. 1336–1614 A.D.

Sanskrit equivalent of Anegondi, an ancient town located on the other side of the river. It was also called Vidyanagara, after Harihara's spiritual adviser Vidyaranya. As the power of the kingdom extended the city came to be identified as Vijayanagara, the city of victory. For almost two and a half centuries, the empire flourished under three dynasties of kings embracing India south of Krishna river.

The political turmoil of South India in the fourteenth century offered favourable opportunities for the rise of a new power. Initially, Srirangapattanam was under the control of Sangama, a Yadava chieftain, who gradually obtained possession of the neighbouring dominions; while his sons Harihara and Bukka were serving as Vodeyas or chieftains of the Hoysala kings. They had displayed exemplary courage in defending Kampili fort against the powerful onslaught of Muhammed Bin Tughlak in 1327 AD, but could not hold it for long. They were taken to Delhi only to be sent back on the condition that they would serve as governors of Kampili for the Sultanate. This implied recognition of their superior prowess which the Sultan would like to avail of to deal with the increasing revolts by the southern kings.

No sooner Harihara and Bukka were able to consolidate Sultan's territories than they were overwhelmed by the spirit of the times, when several viceroys of Deccan were keen to renounce their allegiance to Delhi at the earliest opportunity. They had already seen the surviving example of Jalaluddin Ahsan Shah, who had declared himself in 1334 AD as the sole ruler of Madura, the southernmost province of the Delhi Sultanate. When Tughlak was forced to withdraw his armies to quell a rebellion in the North, it triggered the expected outburst of the simmering revolt in the South. Seizing this moment of advantage in time, Harihara and Bukka declared their independence in 1336 AD. And soon they secured their home base for their future empire by defeating the Hoysala King Vira Ballala III of Dora Samudra. Celebrating his victories, Harihara then established his new capital Vijayanagara. At this time their kingdom extended from Nellore on the south-east coast to Badami on the western side of Deccan.

The emergence of Bahamani kingdom at the northern borders, eleven years later in 1347 AD, did not pose an instant threat; yet the minor Hindu chiefs realised the need to strengthen Vijayanagara and lent their full support. Within a short span of time, most of the country south of river Krishna came under its control. If Vijayanagara owes its birth to Harihara, the credit certainly goes to Bukka for expansion and consolidation of its empire. He was the first ruler to assume the regal title as the king of Vijayanagara in 1356 AD and there were seven more kings of his line who ruled for 150 years.

Sangama dynasty came to an end in 1485 AD, when Narasimha a minister of Saluva family usurped power; and again in 1505 AD the kingdom passed on to the rulers of Tuluva dynasty. Kings of this line, who proved to be men of ability and enterprise, extended their dominions considerably ruling the whole of South India.

Krishna Deva Raya (1510–1529 AD) of this lineage was perhaps the greatest of them all. During the first decade of his rule he consolidated his kingdom, and thereafter in 1520 AD he defeated a coalition of Bahamani forces, who by then were already divided into five separate sultanates. He acquired the much contested Raichur doab, the no man's land between Krishna and Tungabhadra rivers, for which at least ten wars were fought between 1350–1500 AD. He defeated the Gajapathi of Orissa and brought the entire southern peninsula under his control. He maintained mutually advantageous relationship with the Portuguese settlers on the west coast; whereby he retained access to their goods, especially the fine Arabian horses needed for his cavalry, while he allowed them to trade in his territories. During his rule the kingdom became more powerful than before, that was said to be synonymous with military glory, efficient administration, economic prosperity and artistic splendour.

In the later years, there was a gradual disintegration of the empire due to the power struggles among the family members and with the revolting feudatories. Besides, the latter kings had interferred in the politics of the southern Muslim rulers that provoked their enmity which finally induced them to combine against Vijayanagara. In 1565 AD, Rama Raya, an able and ambitious minister, led the empire into a disastrous battle at Rakas-Tangadi (Tallikota), in which the entire army was routed by the combined forces of Bijapur, Ahmadnagar and Golconda; and the capital was plundered and razed to the ground. Tirumala Raya of Aravidu family, however, ruled for a short while from Penukonda; but the kingdom finally collapsed in 1614 AD, though some princes continued as minor chiefs at Vellore and Chandragiri till seventeenth century.

The administrative structure of the kingdom was established by Harihara, borrowing from the Kakatiyas he had served. Madhava, the prime minister of Bukka, carried out several administrative reforms that were continued by later kings. The entire country was formed into convenient administrative units called Sthalas, Nadus, Simas; and the income of the state was increased by reorganisation. The central administration had both revenue side and the military side; and the provincial governors were made responsible for raising taxes. As the central government maintained only a small body of army, the provinces were required to provide troops to the king in proportion to the land they held. Although most of the revenue came from agrarian taxes, commercial and professional taxes were also levied. It was insisted upon that tax should be paid and collected as far as possible in money and not in kind. The mint was improvised, and small

Fig. 9.1 Gold coins of Vijayanagara (electroplated reproductions). 1336–1614 A.D.

denominations of gold and copper coins were issued to enable the farmers to pay their taxes in money.

The currency of Vijayanagara, in conformity with South-Indian tradition, was predominated by gold (Fig. 9.1). 'Varaha', their gold stater, was adopted from the 'Varaha Lanchana' of Western Chalukyas who worshipped Varaha, a reincarnation of Vishnu. It weighed 52 grains, the standard weight of a large kalanju or molucca bean (Caesalpina bonduc). There were also occasional issues of double varaha called 'Doddavaraha'. Evidence from inscriptions indicates the existence of another variety called 'Ghattivaraha' and five such units were said to be equal to seven varahas. Harihara II had issued for the first time half-varaha called after his title as 'Pratapa' or 'Mada' or 'Honnu' and as well a quarter-varaha called 'Kati'. The traditional gold fanam of South India equal to the weight of one manjadi (Adenanthera pavonina) seed was already in circulation; and it was equal to 1/10 of a varaha. The smallest gold coin called 'haga' was also popular in some areas; it weighed 1.3 grains, and its value was reckoned as 1/4 of a gold fanam (Fig. 9.2, 9.3).

No king of Vijayanagara issued silver money except Devaraya; he is said to have issued a small coin called 'Tara' which was equivalent to 1/6 of a gold fanam. Otherwise, the rest of the coinage was in copper, called as 'Pana', 'Jital' and 'Kasu'; and their weight standards and values varied according to regional traditions.

Almost all the coins of Vijayanagara displayed religious symbols on them with the names of the kings on the flip-side. Earlier kings were known to be followers of Saivism, while the later rulers embraced Vaishnavism; yet the devices on their coinage seem to witness their religious tolerance. The Saivite images were limited to Uma and Maheswara, the Vrishabha or bull; and on the other hand the Vaishnavite emblems were numerous: Rama, Hanuman, Garuda, Gandabherunda, Sanka, Chakra, Lakshmi, Lakshmi-Narayana, Varaha, Venkateswara with or without two consorts. Animal figures of power like lion or elephant were also not uncommon.

That the kings of Vijayanagara did not prefer their portraits on their coins is certain; nevertheless they were pleased to impress their names and titles on them. The legends were mostly in Kannada and Nagari scripts. Earlier issues of Harihara and Bukka had Hala (old) Kannada letters in the style of Western Chalukyas and Hoysalas. Coins of Harihara II and Bukka II displayed Nandinagari, while those of the later kings used Devanagari exclusively. A combination of Kannada and Nagari was fancied by Venkata Raya I. Chikka Raya, as an exception, preferred Telugu script on some of his coins, probably for circulation in Andhra territories.

Most of these rulers, in the tradition of Southern kings, were fond of titles and included them on their coins, ordinarily as "Sri Vira (the great warrior) Harihara" or "Sri Vijaya (the victorious) Bukkaraya" or "Sri Pratapa (the most powerful) Krishna Deva Raya". Devaraya I liked novel titles such as "Nilakanta" (one with black neck, Siva), "Uttama" (the best) and "Raja Gajagandabherunda" (the king who is a terror to his enemies as the Gandabherunda is to elephants). Gandabherunda is a mythical double eagle that could hold elephants in each beak and claw. Devaraya II preferred his title as 'Gajabetakara' (hunter of elephants). On the other hand Venkata of the last dynasty included, with all humility, a salutation to his god: 'Venkateswaraya Namah' (adoration to the blessed Venkateswara).

Gold 'Varahas' of Vijayanagara with their high standards of purity and weight became the most acceptable medium of exchange. Portuguese explorer Duarate Barbosa wrote in 1510 AD that "....throughout all India they use this money (varaha) which passes in all those kingdoms". They were also known for their aesthetic appeal, and for this reason some of them have become very popular. The first among them is the 'Uma-Maheswara Varaha' issued by Harihara on which Siva and Parvati were shown sitting side by side. Krishna Deva Raya's 'Durgi Varaha', minted at Chitaldurg, depicting Lord Venkateswara with his Sanka and Chakra was highly sought after. Similar varieties with the effigy of Venkateswara have also become popular such as 'Gandikota Varaha' of Rama Raya and 'Venkatapathi Varaha' of Venkata of the last dynasty. 'Three Swamy Varaha' showing Venkateswara with his two consorts Padmavathi and Alivelu Manga, originally issued by Tirumala Raya, was much imitated later.

The beautiful Varahas of Vijayanagara set a fashion that was followed in subsequent centuries under the name 'Pagoda' by local rulers as well as the European trading companies. The Portuguese traders in India issued as early as 1510 AD their gold 'Cruzodo' of the same size, value and weight as the Varahas so that their money would be acceptable to local traders. They also introduced gold coins called 'pagodas' which were minted at Porto Novo where they had trade settlements. The Dutch United East India Company issued the Tegnapatam gold pagodas with the image of Vishnu on the obverse. They also issued Porto Novo type pagodas which showed Lakshmi on them. The Danish East India Company issued their "C_7" pagodas with the figure of an Indian idol on the reverse.

When the East India Company acquired Madras in 1639–40 AD from the Raja of Chandragiri (probably Venkata III) the terms of lease included permission to mint coins with Vaishnavite symbols like Vishnu, Lakshmi etc. Bound by this agreement, they had issued the famous 'star pagoda' and 'three swamy pagoda'.

On the former type Vishnu was shown, while on the later was Venkateswara with his two consorts. The French East India Company issued 'crescent pagodas' with separate images of Vishnu, Lakshmi and Venkateswara. The Nawabs of Arcot also minted similar pagodas under the names 'Walajahi', 'Kuriki' and 'Umad-ul-Mulki' which had three standing deities on them. All these gold issues weighed around 52 grains and displayed Hindu Pantheon on them. Such was the influence exerted by the gold staters of Vijayanagara.

The flowering of art, literature and architecture that accompanied the material prosperity of Vijayanagara had no parallel in the known history of South India. The most splendid part of the city was the palace enclosure, famous for its temple of Hazara Rama Swamy (the thousand Ramas), its baths and its elephant stables. The artistic granduer of the kingdom was superbly displayed in Virupaksha temple and Krishnaswamy temple. Vittalaswamy temple on the banks of Tungabhadra is perhaps the most wonderous piece of architecture noted for its artistic sculpture and massive construction. It was said to show "the extreme limit in florid magnificence to which the style advances". The great dam at Korragal and the Basavanna Channel were examples of the engineering triumphs of that time.

The city itself grew into a magnificent metropolis of great many wonders, such as the splendorous bazars of diamonds. It attracted several Western travellers who described it in glowing terms. Abder-Razak, the ambassador of Shah Rokh of Persia who visited the city in 1442 AD, greatly admired Vijayanagara: "the city is such that the pupil of the eye has never seen a place like it and the ear of intelligence has never been informed that there existed any thing to equal it in the world". His accounts were confirmed by a Venetian traveller Niccolo-die-Conti who visited the capital in the early part of fifteenth century and also by Caesar Frederick who saw it three years after its fall. Such sensuously evocative descriptions, though seem exaggerated, are perhaps more appropriate for visualising the glory that was Vijayanagara.

Fig. 10.1 Viraraya fanams, very small ancient South Indian gold coins (obverse).

10. THE GOLDEN SOUTH

Nature's bounty of gold in Southern India is well known; and even today the South remains to be India's prime source of this precious metal, with its mines at Kolar, Hutti and other places. As if this was not enough, plenty of gold found its way to the South for centuries as a result of thriving foreign trade. Ancient Tamil Sangam literature attests to the prosperity of Yavana (Greek) merchants trading in towns such as Kaveripattinam. Excavations at Arikamedu revealed that there was once a Roman trading settlement of 1st and 2nd centuries AD. Several hordes of gold

Fig. 10.2 Viraraya fanams, very small ancient South Indian gold coins (reverse).

coins of Roman emperors, of first Century AD., Augustus, Tiberius and Nero were found at ancient trading centres or sources of precious stones. As the balance of trade was in favour of India, Romans had paid in gold coins for the luxury items, pepper, silk, ivory, pearls and gems like quartz, beryl and diamonds. The fact that these were found overstruck with a bar suggests that they were used as bullion in Southern India.

The South is so fabulous for its gold that every conqueror collected it to his heart's content. Ferista, a Persian chronicler, tells that in 1310–11 AD, Malik Kafur, on his return to Delhi, presented his sovereign Alla-Uddin Mohammed with the plunder he brought from the South that included 96,000 maunds of gold alone. He states further that "no person wore bracelets, chains or rings of any other metal than gold; while all the plates in the houses of the great and in the temples were of beaten gold". Again, after Mohammed Bin Tughlaq's successful campaigns in Deccan, there was such a great influx of gold to Delhi that its market value fell very sharply, and as a consequence the people were reluctant to accept the official gold dinar as its intrinsic value had been reduced. To correct the situation it has been said that the sultan had taken the unusual measure of increasing the weight of dinar from 170 to 201.6 grains (11.02 to 13.06 gm). Such were the tales connected with the southern gold. In fact, the currency continued to be mainly of gold until the Mohammedans came to be permanently established in the South.

The gold fanam, the smallest unit of southern currency, derives its name from the word 'Pan' that rhymes with the Sanskrit word 'Ran'. Dr. Caldwell in his 'Comparative Grammar' included 'Pana' in the list of the words which are the "common property of Sanskrit and Dravidian tongues". The root 'Pan' (to make, to work, to produce) is undoubtedly a primitive Dravidian element; but 'Panam' (money) is deduced by Dravidian grammarians from the Sanskrit root 'Pan' (to do business), a subtle distinction. But it is more likely that the origin of the word is Dravidian.

A piece of gold used as a medium of exchange is always reckoned in terms of a predetermined weight. The Southern metric system appears to have been founded on seminal weights of native seeds, for weighing gems, gold and pearls. A nen-mani (a grain of rice in husk) served as the lowest weight called Visa. 4 nel served as the next higher weight called Kunri (or rati); while 2 Kunri are counted as one Manjadi. 10 Manjadi are equal to one Kalanju, of the highest weight.

Thus the whole system is based mainly on two seeds. Manjadi is a small seed of a common tree (Adenanthera pavonina). Hard and durable, it is scarlet in colour. Its name is said to have been taken from the form of the beans that are shaped like Manjuzhi, a kind of boat, so common in South. The average weight of the seed is 4.5 to 5 grains (0.292 to 0.324 gm). Since no seeds are equal in weight, the inconvenience is rectified over a period of time by substituting metallic weights; and Pana was the representative of Manjadi. 'Kalanju' (Karanju or Kazhanju) is the seed of a prickly climbing species of Caesalpina (Guilandina bonduc). In Hindi it is called Nata-Karanja and in Telugu, Gachakai. These grey seeds are hard and smooth. The mature ones average 45 to 50 grains (2.915 to 3.24 gm). The scales used for weighing precious stones are named after this seed as Kalanju-kol. A standard gold coin is often called a Kalanju as its weight is equal to that of the seed. The tenth part is called 'Panam' or 'fanam' as its weight is that of a 'Manjadi'.

The Southern gold coinage has independent development but it is difficult to trace its origin. The oldest known coins are the plain and smooth spherules that often have a punch mark too small to be identified. They weigh 52 grains (3.368 gm), evidently derived from 'Kalanju'. Their original name is 'Pon' which in Tamil simply means gold. While it became 'Hon' in Kannada, the later Mohammedan rulers called it 'Hun'. This kind of money appears to have been in use for a long time.

Some of the ancient punch-marked gold coins were found beyond the limits of India proper, in the island of Ramree, obviously the result of a ship-wreck. They were thin and circular nearly an inch and a half in diameter, weighing 66 grains. The figure of a boar at the centre points to their Chalukyan origin. Large and rude letters impressed around the periphery correspond to a script that was in vogue during 5th and 6th centuries AD. Tavernier, a French traveller who visited Southern India during 17th century AD, described some primitive coins that included a cup-shaped one with a single punch mark of Hanuman; on the convex reverse it showed in relief a lion looking backwards, the symbol of the Kadambas.

The emergence of 'Padma Tanakas' or 'Kamala Mudras' marks the second stage. They are flat, round, and thick pieces of skilful workmanship. At the centre is seen a lotus, a favourite emblem of the Jains. It is surrounded by four punch marks struck afterwards. These marks appeared initially on the obverse only, but later they were impressed on both sides. These weigh a little more than a Kalanju; and certainly they were heavier than, 'Pon' or 'Hun' which in course of time became general as Varaha or Pagoda. The superior execution of Padmatanakas ruled for a considerable time with many variations, until the adaptation of matrix or double-die led to the final disuse of punch.

Finally, the modern die-struck gold coins arrived under the name of Pagodas or Huns. The early issues showed a floral design; and rightly they are called Phuli-Huns (flowery Pagodas). They appear to have been generally adopted by many. It is found on Chalukya and Chera coins, with a symbol of a seat or couch on some kind of edifice. The 'Hun' of Bijapur has a heart-shaped symbol on the obverse. Some of them have the Persian letters 'ain' and 'sin' impressed on the symbol, which are assigned to Adil-Shah dynasty who recirculated the old coins of the previous native rulers, after punching these additional marks. The Pagodas of later date showed perfect obverse and reverse.

Most of the Southern Pagodas fall into three principal types. The first has a standing figure of Sri Venkateswara (Vishnu), the deity at Tirupathi. This appears to have been derived from the Vaishnava faiths of the later Vijayanagara princes of Chandragiri and chiefs of Venkatagiri. This variety is adopted by the East India Company in their Star Pagoda; and as well by the Portuguese in their Porto Novo Pagoda. The Nawabs of Arcot also imitated it on their Huns. The next group is that of Durga Pagodas, which showed a seated goddess Durga on the obverse, with the letters Sri Pratapa in Nagari script on the reverse. These are known by various prefixes, such as Durga, Gurramkonda, Hardanahalli, Chitaldurgi, Dharwari, Sravanore, etc. Most of them were current in the districts

Fig. 10.3 A small gold coin of Krishnaraja Wodeyar of Mysore (obverse) with Uma and Maheswara.

of Cuddapah (A.P.) and Bellary (Karnataka). Many of them have Vaishnava symbols of Sanka (Conch) and Chakra (Wheel). The third variety has the effigies of Siva and Parvathi, and they are popularly known as Uma-Maheswara Pagodas. Minted at lkkeri and Bednur, they were in circulation in Mysore state. Wodeyars of Mysore issued similar gold coins in different denominations (Fig. 10.3).

Gradually the gold coinage evolved to exhibit more definite devices, with legends in Hala-Kannada (Old Kannada) and Nagari characters. The coins became narrower and thicker, but without alteration of the standard weight of 52 grains. Half Pagodas were also issued, under various names such as 'Pratapa' or 'Mada' or 'Honnu'. They showed the same devices as the full-sized Pagoda. Similarly they were repeated on the gold fanams which are equivalent to 1/10 of a Pagoda, weighing 5 to 6 grains (0.292 to 0.324 gm).

The origin of small gold fanams is traced to the religious belief that it is auspicious to give away gold as 'daksina' to Brahmin priests. Quoting from

Fig. 10.4 A small gold coin of Krishnaraja Wodeyar of Mysore (reverse) with Nagari legend *Sri Krishna Raja.*

Krishna Yajurveda, R. Srinivasa Raghava Ayyangar tells an interesting story in an article titled 'Ancient South Indian Gold Coinage' in Indian Historical Quarterly (111, 1-1927). According to epics, silver was formed out of the tears of Agni as a result of beating by Devas, when he tried to appropriate their gold treasures. It is believed that it is inauspicious to give away silver as daksina lest an inauspicious event should visit the house within a period of one year. As Vedas forbid giving away silver it became a matter of necessity to offer gold in all religious ceremonies; and this tradition continued for centuries in Southern India.

In order that gold might be accessible both to the rich and the poor, southern kings have minted small denominations of gold fanams and made available to people to enable them to use in religious offerings. Even the Moghul emperors like Aurangzeb, Farrukhsiyar, Mohammad Shah and Alamgir II realized the need for small gold coins and issued half fanams for local circulation from their southern mints at Gutti, Tadipathri and Cuddapah.

The fanams connected with the principal dynasties of Southern India depict the emblems as on their Huns or Pagodas. The elephants are seen on fanams of Coorg; the presence of boar is typical of Chalukyas; the Kadamba issues have a lion looking back; and the fish and tiger appear on the Chola-Chalukya coinage. Some of them show gods or goddesses such as we see on Lakshmi fanam. Due to lack of space on the diminutive coins, legends rarely appear. The name of the king appears on the fanams of Shivaji, Rama Raya and Mohammedan rulers. Sometimes one letter is seen as in Tippu Sultan's fanams.

Many of these fanams of incredible beauty have peculiar symbols, without legends, that are difficult to explain. Very common fanams of this variety that once passed among the sarafs as Ratiraval or Viraraya fanams, deserve some attention (Fig. 10.1, 10.2). They offer no clue as to their origin. Some scholars believe that they emanated from Coorg or Bednur; yet some others assign them to Zamorin who ruled the Malabar coast after the partition of Kerala. But then, how to account for their general distribution in the eastern districts? It is explained that in the areas of Palaghat and Cherkal the exchange of Pagoda for Viraraya fanam was very variable fluctuating between 11.25 to 11.75 per cent, so that a profit margin of 11 to 12 per cent is gained by bringing Pagodas from Karnataka and carrying back Viraraya fanams. It is also probable that their prevalence in Andhra desa, Karnataka and Tamilnadu may have prompted imitations to facilitate local currency; and this would account for the variations observed.

The curious devices add subtle grace to these little pieces of gold, as can be seen on the three coins shown here. According to one scholar the indistinct lines on the obverse appear to be remnants of an effaced Sanka (conch): a sort of oblong or elongated mark could be the remains of a degraded standing figure. The symbols on the reverse defy every attempt to give them an intelligible meaning. They exhibit a transverse bar, sometimes the end turned like the letter 'J' or simply elongated something like a crocodile or saurian. Sometimes one or two dependent lines are seen, after which the money changers have named them as single plough or double plough fanams. Above this, there are always a number of dots arranged in two or three lines over each other. Another scholar compared this to a Jinjal, a wall piece of ordnance with a pile of shot. Similar symbols appear on the gold rasi of Travancore and on the silver Mangalore fanams. The significance of these symbols is not clearly known.

One may think that the small size of the gold fanam would have rendered its use inconvenient. On the contrary, they were further minimized as is evident from the tiny pieces which weigh from 1 to 2.5 grains. They may be taken to represent quarter and half fanams. The Kadambas issued half fanams weighing 2.9 grains; and the Rajahs of Travancore also issued Chinna fanams weighing 2.8 grains. Some of the smallest ones are known for their purity, and as such they deserve the name Aparanji fanam by which they are sometimes called. They are often found on old sites after heavy rains.

Thus, the South has the distinction of minting minute coins of gold initially for religious purposes and later for the convenience of small transactions of trade, contrary to the universal practice of using cheaper metals like silver or copper for smaller denominations. It is a phenomenon found nowhere else in the world. More than the belief in gold, it is the demonstration of real value of money. It is true that the *el dorado* of the south has faded into history, but it lives on forever through the legends of the folklore. Its surviving artifacts, the gold fanams, bear silent witness to its past glory.

Fig. 11.1 A medal of East India Company (obverse) with Shah Alam's regnal year 19, and Murshidabad mint mark. Around 1835 A.D. (Top)
Fig. 11.2 A medal of East India Company (reverse). (Below)

11. THOSE MAGNIFICENT MEDALS*

The medal today is a universal phenomenon. There is one for every occasion. At the very sight of this embodiment of honour, spirits soar high. And when it comes to giving or receiving one, everyone is pleased without exception.

Its name is derived from 'medaille', a French word for metal. It is a piece of metal issued to commemorate a person, place or event. Ranging from a large medallion to a small plaque, it can take any form such as a cross or star, though the shape of a disc is the most common one.

Most medals are made of gold, silver, bronze or any other metal or alloy. Earlier they were cast from a model of wax, wood or stone; or made by die-striking method, using a handcut die. A few of them are produced by the 'repousse' process; where two thin flans of silver, one for each side, are hammered from the reverse into a design of raised relief; and both are soldered later to a silver rim.

Examples of Roman medallions of bronze and other metals commemorating events in history are well known. Alexander the Great is said to have issued a medal to mark his victories, the sole example of which is in the British Museum. It is generally accepted that the art of the medallist began in 1438 A.D. with a bronze medal of the Byzantine emperor John VII Palaeologus, the first of a series of portrait medals. It was the invention of an Italian painter Antonio Pisano, called Pisanello. His medal provided a miniature portrait relief of a person, reproducible by casting in lead or bronze. Its size is small enough to be held on the palm and elegant enough to be worn as an ornament. He placed a profile portrait on the obverse and an allegorical or pictorial scene on the reverse. This formula for the medal has lasted till today. With the development of major schools of medal making towards the end of the 15th century, the portrait effigy became more sculptural and bolder.

---

*Courtesy: The Hindu. This article was published by the author under the title 'Those magnificent medals' in The Hindu dated 12-10-1991.

Fine works of art in medallic form were produced by artists of Italian renaissance and others that followed. The cast medal of Michelangelo by Leone Leoni is a masterpiece. A portrait medal of bronzegilt of Henry IV and Marie de Medicis by Guillaume Dupre is absolutely charming. The famous medal of Erasmus by Quentin Massys is said to be the grandest medal of northern renaissance. A gold medal of Robert Dudley, the Earl of Leicester, created by Hendrik Goltzius is an excellent example of engraving skill. The fineness of the art can be seen in the Francois Briot's medal of Louis XIII.

Talented medallists were highly sought after, and were even favoured with court appointments under royal patronage. The Italian medalist Antonio Abondio was appointed as Court Medalist by Maximilian II in Prague. The Swiss medallist Johann Carl Hedlinger was similarly honoured in Stockholm. Germain Pilon was appointed as 'Controleur General des Effigies'. Guillaume Dupre was given total control of the Paris mint. Leone Leoni was respected as Court Sculptor to Charles V. Benevenuto Cellini was blessed to be an exclusive medallist for the Pope. Great medallists of the 18th and 19th centuries include Benedetta Pitrucci in Italy, Hubert Ponscarme and Jules-Clement Chaplain in France and John Crocker and the Wyon family in England.

The struck medal became a common instrument of Court propaganda for Popes and the Ruling Medici family of Florence in the 16th century. Henry II of France released numerous propaganda medals. Netherlands produced several such pieces as vehicles of national sentiment. The Dutch wars with France and England stimulated many issues depicting political events of the time. To commemorate his reign Louis XIV had commissioned a grand series of 'Histoire Metallique' (history in metal). A similar elaborate series was ordered by the Napoleonic regime.

The propaganda medal is short-lived though its influence can be felt even today, when we examine some of the slogans appearing on recent coins: 'Grow more food'; 'Planned families and food for all'; 'Food and shelter for all'; 'Save for development'; 'National integration', etc. A metal token attached to key-chains—with corporate monograms and product messages, often distributed by modern advertisers, is another reincarnation of the propaganda medal.

The custom of awarding medals for participation in war or service to the nation was introduced in England during the time of Henry VIII. The Armada Medal commemorating the defeat of the Spanish Armada in 1588 was given by Elizabeth I as a reward for the British soldiers. It was intended to be worn as an ornament. The awards for bravery and service were made for the first time in 1794 when the British defeated the French in the Atlantic.

The regular system of decorating the survivors of actions on land and sea was introduced in 1848 by the Queen Victoria. Even the East India Company decorated some of its servants with medals suspended from ribands (Fig. 11.1, 11.2).

In India, service to the nation is honoured by the supreme award of 'Bharat Ratna'. 'Padma Vibhushan', 'Padma Bhushan' and 'Padma Sri' are the special honours awarded to eminent persons of all walks of life in recognition of their achievements. Bravery and active service in the face of enemy are honoured by awarding 'Param Vir Chakra'. The 'Param Visisht Seva Medal' is the highest during the peace time. The highest award of 'Ashok Chakra' is awarded to civilians for displaying bravery. In recognition of the distinguished or meritorious services, the President of India awards several other medals to deserving service personnel—separately for Army, Navy, Air Force, Police, Coast Guard, etc. For life saving and bravery, there are special awards for children.

Medal making saw new developments in the later centuries as could be seen in the refined works of Pierre-Jean David D'Angers and Benjamin Duvivier who combined the Rococo elegance with realism. With the development of steam-powered press by Mathew Boulton, large scale medal production became possible. During the reign of William IV and Victoria the commemorative medal reached its zenith.

An immense background history lies behind every medal.

Fig. 12.1 British War Medal, Victory Medal (WW-I) and Burma Medal (obverse).

Fig. 12.2 British War Medal (WW-I), Victory Medal and Burma Medal (reverse).

12. HISTORY IN METAL

Let us consider some rare medals that are historically significant. The Burma medal was issued by East India Company which came into existence in 1599 with merchant adventurers in London joining hands to trade with the Far East. Gradually over a period of 300 years, the Company assumed the power and proportions of imperial magnificence. From 1778, when the Company issued its first medal, it had made a custom for many years of issuing campaign and service medals, acknowledging the services of its troops, long before the British Government realized the necessity of issuing such tokens in 1816.

Burma medal (Fig. 12.1, 12.2) is classified under India General Service Medal 1854-95. It was instituted in 1854 to commemorate the British campaigns in Burma between 28th March, 1852 and 30th June 1853. The war was the result of repeated acts of aggression by Burmese governors on the borders adjacent to Company's territories. This in turn brought the Company into conflict with the neighbouring countries as well as the French and other nations which claimed territories.

Unlike several of the earlier Indian medals this medal was not issued without a bar; there were 23 bars awarded, but the maximum number of bars to one medal appears to be seven. On the obverse Britannia is placing an olive wreath on the head of a seated soldier, while the crowned queen is depicted on the reverse with the legend VICTORIA REGINA. The letters BURMA 1887-89 are prominently visible on the bar of the medal, while the name and the regiment of the recipient were engraved on its edge. This indeed is a memento of recognition of courage and valour displayed by an Indian soldier in a British campaign.

Medals of the First and Second World Wars are sought after by collectors the world over. Among the war medals the award of a medallion is very uncommon. Here is The Great War Memorial plaque, measuring 12 cm across, posthumously awarded to an Indian soldier (Fig. 12.7). It was given to next of kin. Around the medallion appear the words HE DIED FOR FREEDOM AND HONOUR. Britannia, standing beside a lion, holding a trident in one hand and an olive

Fig. 12.3 Delhi Coronation Durbar Medal, The Defence Medal (WW-II) and Independence of India Medal (obverse).

wreath in the other is blessing the name MUNISAMI. Unlike medals which depict the effigy of King or Queen, the other side of this medallion is blank.

In general practice, the required number of medals are cast from a single die and then the name and particulars of the recipient are engraved separately on the edge of each medal. However, in the case of this medallion the name of the soldier was included as part of the original die; and it is obvious that this was the only piece made out of that special die. That indeed makes it a special award. Speaking of this series of medals, Edward C. Joslin of Spink & Son Ltd., London, says in The Observer's Book of British Awards and Medals' that these bronze issues are scarce, as indeed are all issues with the head of George V.

One such rare example is the British War Medal (WWI) issued in silver (Fig. 12.1, 12.2). It has the portrait of George V on the obverse with a legend surrounding it, while the reverse shows St. George on horseback being in the process of trampling on the shield of Central Powers. At the foot is a skull and cross bones with a rising sun above. Around the edge are dates 1914-1918. The name of the recipient is engraved on the edge. This medal commemorated some of the most terrible battles ever known, the casualties being astronomical.

Victory Medal 1914–18, issued in bronze, is another rare example (Fig. 12.1, 12.2). It was awarded only to those who received 1914 or 1914-15 medal and to

Fig. 12.4 Delhi Coronation Durbar Medal, The Defence Medal (WW-II) and Independence of India Medal (reverse).

most of those who were awarded the British medal described above. It was never awarded singly. To qualify, one had to be mobilized in any of the British Services between 5 August 1914 and 11 November 1918. The obverse contained the inscription THE GREAT WAR FOR CIVILISATION 1914-1919, within an oak wreath, and on the reverse the portrait of Victory is depicted.

The Defence Medal (3 Sept 1939–2 Sept 1945) is the commonest among the medals of the Second World War, but it is rare to find these days (Fig. 12.3, 12.4). It was awarded for three years' service in Britain or for six months' service in non-operational area which was subjected to or closely threatened by air attack. The obverse shows the British Crown on the stump of an oak tree flanked by two lions with the dates '1939-1945' at the top and in the exergue THE DEFENCE MEDAL. King George VI is depicted on the reverse with the legend GEORGIUS VI. D:G: BR: OMN:REX.FD: IND: IMP. It was awarded in cupro-nickel, although the Canadian issue was in silver. The riband was very symbolical, the green representing the British isles, the orange flames, the bombing and the black, the black out during war.

The emblem of silver laurel leaves was granted to civilians other than those in the Merchant Navy to denote King's commendation for brave conduct during the Second World War 1939-45. This emblem is worn on the riband of the Defence Medal.

Fig. 12.5 Commemorative Medal of Queen Victoria's Hanover visit 1837 (obverse) with uncrowned head of the Queen.

Fig. 12.6 Commemorative Medal of Queen Victoria's Hanover visit 1837 (reverse) with St. George riding a horse.

On the occasion of India's independence the British mint had issued a commemorative medal (Fig. 12.3, 12.4). Ashoka's Lion Capital is depicted on the obverse with the surrounding legend INDIAN INDEPENDENCE 15th AUGUST, 1947. On the reverse Ashoka Chakra takes the central position with a small British Crown above. The legend reads: GEORGIUS VI. DG: BRITT.OMN: REX: MD: DBP. This indicates that India gained independence during the reign of King George VI. This medal was awarded to all Indian Soldiers on this important occasion. The absence of the letters IND: IMP in the legend is conspicuous, because King George VI was no longer the emperor of India.

British medals were struck not only to commemorate State occasions but also the official visits of the King and the Queen. In this tradition a medal was issued commemorating the royal visit of Alexandrina Victoria, the Queen of Great Britain, to Hanover in 1837. A lot of history lies behind this medal.

Queen Victoria had the lineage of the House of Hanover, which supplied five British Monarchs between 1714 and 1837. Her grandfather George III and uncle William IV both hailed from this royal family. Her mother, Victoria Mary Luisa, was the daughter of the duke of Saxe-Saalfeld-Coburg of Hanover. The Queen's consort prince Albert, son of Earnest I, belonged to the royal house of Saxe-Coburg-Gotha of Hanover. This German name of the royal family was changed to Windsor during the reign of George V.

Victoria inherited the British throne when William IV died on 20 June 1837, and was crowned on 28 June 1838. Since the Salic law prevented succession by a woman, she could not become the Queen of Hanover. As a result the crowns of Great Britain and Hanover were separated, and the latter passed to Earnest August, the eldest surviving brother of William IV. Immediately after the Queen's accession but before coronation, she paid a royal visit to Hanover in 1837. On this occasion commemorative medals were struck in gold for members of the royal family and principal overseas representatives, in silver for officers and in bronze for other ranks (Fig. 12.5, 12.6). The medal depicts an uncrowned portrait of the Queen with the legend VICTORIA QUEEN OF GREAT BRITAIN. On the reverse the words 'TO HANOVER' appear with the date 1837. St. George is shown riding a horse above the skeleton of a two-headed dragon pi-ohahlv symbolising the end of the House of Hanover.

The Delhi Coronation Durbar Medal reminds us of one of the important events in Indian history. King George V (George Frederick Earnest Albert) was coronated on 221 June 191 as the King of Great Britain and Emperor of India. Thereafter he visited India and held the Coronation Durbar in Delhi on 12 December 1911. It was an event which appealed to the imagination of India and her traditional spirit of reverence for kingship. The enthusiasm with which the King and the queen were received far exceeded then expectations, often in the form of almost semi-devine worship.

On both occasions of coronation in London and Delhi, the British mint issued commemorative medals. On Delhi Coronation Durbar Medal the royal crown was placed above the date 12th December, 1911 (Fig. 12.3, 12.4); on the reverse the king and queen were depicted with the legend GEORGE V and MARY. This cupro-nickel variety was probably issued for distribution to general public. This medal was also issued in gold for Ruling Chiefs of India.

On this important occasion the king announced the revocation of Lord Curzon's partition of Bengal. The Bengal province was resettled with the creation of a new province of Bihar and Orissa, which was supposed to heal the Hindu population's old sores of Lord Curzon's partition. Another important decision was announced to transfer the capital from Calcutta to Delhi the ancient seat of Moghul empire, which was chiefly intended to gratify Mohammedan sentiment.

Fig. 13.1 Coins struck on different metals other than the one used for regular issues (obverse). (Top)

Fig. 13.2 Coins struck on different metals other than the one used for regular issues (reverse). (Below)

13. A PASTIME GAINING CURRENCY*

It is a classic case of how keeping up with Joneses can lead to ruin. Inspired by Chinese emperor Kublai Khan's successful introduction of paper currency as the sole medium of exchange throughout his realm, Mohammed Bin Tughlak decided to do even better.

In 1329 AD, Tughlak substituted silver and gold coinage with brass and metal tokens inscribed "He who obeys the Sultan obeys the Compassionate" expecting it to compel public acceptance. The fiat was one Tughlak was destined to rue. But it is one for which numismatists today are thankful.

The adage, that 'old is gold', perhaps best fits the popular hobby of coin collecting. The only catch is that very few old coins survive the test of time. Take the case of Tughlak's coins. Virtually overnight, houses in Tughlak's kingdom were converted into mini mints and these cheap metal tokens were churned out in thousands.

The obvious failure of the scheme forced the king to withdraw the entire coinage at his own cost three years after its introduction. And silver *tankahs* from the treasury were exchanged for genuine as well as spurious tokens. Very few of them survive today and have become collector's items.

While some coins are withdrawn from circulation, others become worn out due to rubbing. A few, though, do remain in mint condition. And while every rare coin is beautiful for a collector, a beautiful coin is even rarer. Because a beautiful coin adds more to its value than its antiquity.

Even so, a rare coin, however beautiful, is not worth its metal unless it attracts a collector, who may be looking for a wide variety of coins for many different reasons. He could be on the look-out for a 'key' coin within a given series, such as the Indian rupee of 1939, required to complete a set. Or he may be searching for a fascinating piece like the commemorative medal of Alexander the Great. In

---

*Courtesy: The Economic Times. This article was published by the author under the title 'A pastime gaining currency' in The Economic Times, dated 21-9-1991.

most cases, the value depends on limited availability. In fact, nothing is rarer than a single specimen of its kind.

The most important factor that contributes to the rarity of a coin is its mintage—the total number of coins manufactured in a given year. It follows, therefore, that the lower the mintage, the higher its value.

Survival is also very important. Coins disappear for various reasons. A few, like the rupee coin of the East India Company dated 1834 with the obverse of William IV, were never released for circulation. There are also instances when whole currencies were withdrawn from circulation due to demonetisation or some other reason—like in the case of Tughlak's folly.

A rather bizarre and unfortunate cause for the disappearance of vintage coins was created by the hike in silver prices few weeks ago. Many rare coins ended up in the melting pot to be converted into bullion!

While rarity may be an important factor that determines the value of a coin, perhaps equally important is the popularity (or notoriety) with collectors. This raises the demand for such pieces, and also pushes up the premium on them.

The best examples of such coins are what can be called the 'rejects'. Though most rejects are returned for re-melting due to the strict rules of mints, some find their way into collector's hands. Such oddities command their own price.

Mistakes usually occur because wrong planchet (a metal disc from which coins are made)—intended for another denomination of the same metal—is used for coin. If a planchet of double thickness is used, the resultant coin is called a 'pie-fort', which is naturally bulkier than the circulation issues. On the other hand, the use of a planchet of the wrong metal may result in a novel piece called 'off-metal-strike'.

A classic example is the silver off-metal-strike of gold mohur issued by the East India Company for circulation in Bombay Presidency. Since its rim is slightly trimmed, the diameter of the coin is less than that of the original mohur (Fig. 13.1, 13.2). This is an interesting coin. On the obverse side is a Persian legend with the date 1748 AD—common to the issues of the Sultan Azizuddin Alamgir II. The flip side bears a legend in English with floral ornamentation: 'Bombay 1770 15 Rups'. Though the sultan died in 1759 AD, this gold coin was issued posthumously in his name. This particular off-metal-strike is quite rare but is yet to find a place in world coin catalogues.

There are also cases of counterfeit coins deceptively passed off as off-metal-strikes. However, they can usually be spotted by the trained eye. Silvered brass coins put into circulation are a good example (Fig. 13.1, 13.2). Due to wear and tear, the silver coating is often rubbed off thus exposing the original brass. One could easily mistake them for off-metal-strikes of silver half-rupees. But while the real pieces of this variety are immaculate in their appearance—without any trace of wear—the well worn surfaces of these coins give away their dubious history.

Another common error among rejects results from the use of improper dies. While the correct planchet is employed, the dies on the two sides may not match each other. This produces a hybrid coin called a mule (because the mules are said to have the head of horse and the body of a donkey).

Several varieties of striking errors can result due to this mismatch. An interesting combination results when an off-centre-piece ends up with a blank space as the die has been partly impressed on the planchet. When struck again on the missing area, the impression often overlaps, resulting in a clip coin. And if there is more than one strike, it culminates in a set of errors known as double-strikes, multi-strikes or over-strikes.

There is yet another breed of rarities—those created by intent. These are quite different from mint-errors which acquire this status by accident. During the 18th and 19th centuries a few such pieces—called box-coins—were produced. They were coins which had been hollowed out or made from two coins machined to fit together, in which something could be hidden. An example of this variety were Britain's big, clunky two-pence copper of 1797.

Identifying such flaws is, perhaps, one of the most interesting aspects of numismatics. Indeed, there are collectors specialising only in imperfect coins. But for an increasing number of people who have taken up this fascinating hobby, coin collecting is simply an indelible impression of history.

Fig. 14.4 A silver coin of Kuninda.
Obverse: With the Sanskrit legend *Rajna Kunindasa Amoghabhuthasa Maharajasa.*
Reverse: Same legend in Kharoshti script.

14. FASCINATING RARITIES

Looking for numismatic rarities is fascinating as well as exciting. Fascinating because it stimulates one's imagination, and absolutely exciting, when one owns a priceless piece. The thrill of this hobby lies in one's success in decoding an unidentified coin. The moment the mystery of an unusual find is unfolded, its hidden beauty comes alive. The delightful sight of such a wonderful thing is simply arresting, and its possession indeed is a joy for ever. Some prior knowledge is helpful but certainly not a prerequisite. Any one who stumbles up on an old curiosity can always discover its true identity by looking up various catalogues and literature. Searching for the elusive rarities is an enchanting experience worth pursuing. Let us consider some rare coins from the author's collection.

Fig. 14.3 A potin coin of Srimukha Sata with Sanskrit legend *Srimuka Sata* (obverse) and faint Ujjain symbol (reverse). 3rd Century B.C.

There is an extraordinary interest the world over in ancient coins with the image of Alexander the Great. Having conquered a large part of the world he entertained thoughts of his own divinity and insisted on its acceptance by others. Many countries, perforce, yielded rather reluctantly. Sparta complied ironically saying "since Alexander wishes to be a god, let him be a god'. When the Macedonian conqueror died in 323 BC, his generals divided the empire among themselves.

Ptolemy I in Egypt (323-285 BC) with due respect to his master broke all traditions by showing the likeness of an actual person, the deified Alexander, on his tetradrachms. Lysimachus, a trusted general who became the king of Thrace after Alexander in 306 BC, also issued a tetradrachm (a silver coin) with an idealized head of the divine conqueror, on which Alexander is wearing the horn of the Egyptian ram-god Ammon, a symbol of immortality. Ammon is believed to be an incarnation of the Greek god Zeus. On the reverse the Greek goddes Athena was seated blessing the name of the king. The demand for the coins with the portrait of Alexander is so much that a large number of imitations have come up for sale (Fig. 14.1, 14.2). Sometimes it is difficult to say which one is genuine. The romantic appeal of these coins is such that some collectors like to possess even the spurious ones.

Here is another piece of historical importance, that of Srimukha the first king of Andhras who were settled in third century BC in the land between Krishna and Godavari rivers (Fig. 14.3). Kings of the Andhra dynasty were listed in five puranas—Matsya, Vayu, Brahmanda, Vishnu and Bhagavatha. Matsya purana gives a complete list of 29 kings, assigning them a rule of 460 years. Most of the puranas agree that the first king of Andhras rose to power by slaying Susurman the last of the Kanvas. Historians believe that Srimukha asserted his independence soon after the death of Ashoka in 232 BC. His son Satakarni expanded the kingdom that included all the land south of Vindhyas; and he was aptly called the Dakshinapathapathi (Lord of Deccan). Andhras ruled for four and a half centuries probably from 220 BC to 220 AD, with three capitals at Dhanyakataka (Dharanikota) near Amaravathi, Guntur Dist., A.P., Prathishtana or modern Paithan, Aurangabad Dist., Maharashtra, and Vijayanthi or modern Banavasi in North Canara Dist., Karnataka.

King Srimukha is variously described in Puranas as Sipraka, Sindhuka and Sisuka. Historians conclude that this variation is due to accumulated errors of generations of scribes and consequent corruption in manuscripts. In Bhagavatha he is described as 'Vrasalo Bali' (a strong sudra). His non-ksathriya origin indicates that he probably descended from some foreign invaders. In Nanaghat inscription of Naganika wife of Satakarni, he is described as Simuka Satavahana. Legends on his coins indicate that he was called Chimuka. Simuka and Chimuka

Fig. 14.7 A silver coin of Kumara Gupta (obverse) with the portrait of the king with some Greek letters behind the head. 413–455 A.D.

Fig. 14.8 A silver coin of Kumara Gupta (reverse) with Garuda symbol and Sanskrit legend *Parama Bhagavatha Maharajadhiraja Sri Kumara Gupta Mahendraditya.*

are perhaps the Prakrit versions of the Sanskrit name Srimukha, just as Satavahana is the Prakrit for Swethavahana. In this rare coin of the king, the legend is in Brahmi characters. The first letter is not very clear but the latter four letters are quite legible, and it reads *Srimuka Sata*. On the reverse two arms of the Ujjain symbol are faintly visible.

Coins of Andhra dynasty were thoroughly studied by E.J. Rapson, professor of Sanskrit at Cambridge University, London, and a scholar of Indian numismatics. It is indeed surprising to note that there was not a single coin of Srimukha among 236 Andhra coins in the British Museum catalogued by him. In all probability this was due to the scarcity of Srimukha's coins. One can imagine how important is this rare piece of evidence for historians.

Kuninda silver coins are perhaps the most beautiful ones issued by the Indian kings during the first century BC. Kunindas were tribal kings who occupied the hilly tracts near the river Sutlez in Indus region. A large number of Kuninda coins were found in the country between Ambala and Saharanpur. Sir Cunningham says that their capital might have been at Srugna (or Sugh) on the west bank of the old Jamuna where the high road from Punjab to the eastward crossed the

TI.CLAVDIVS CAESAR AVG.P.M.TR.P.IMP

Fig. 14.6 A coin of Tiberius Caesar (reverse) almost flat with indistinct symbol and the letters S and C. 1st Century A.D.

Fig. 14.5 A coin of Tiberius Caesar with the legend TI. CLAVDIVS CAESAR. AVG. PM. TRP. IMP. and the portrait of the king (obverse). 1st Century A.D. (a fake coin).

river for many centuries. In the example shown here (Fig. 14.4), the name of the king *'Rajna Kunindasa Amoghabhuthasa Maharajasa'* is written in Brahmi characters on one side and in Kharoshti letters on the other. A standing figure of a female holding flowers in front of a deer depicted on the obverse indicates the king's commitment to the principle of 'ahimsa'. His title 'Amoghabhuthasa' means lover of animals. Just below is a three-arched 'chaitya', probably the emblem of Mauryas under whom the Kunindas were once feudatories. Just above the animal is another uncertain symbol. On the reverse appear five symbols, Kushana emblem of 'nandipada', a swastika, a six-arched chaitya, a tree in railing and another uncertain symbol. A wavy line below probably indicates the river of the country to which the coin belongs. This coin belongs to an earlier type modelled after the Indo-Greek coins of that period. The later types have a trident and battle-axe of Siva without the tribal name. The clarity of legends and symbols and the meticulous care with which it was executed makes it a piece worth possessing.

Another interesting piece, shown here, is picked up by the author from a roadside vendor. It has the portrait of the Roman emperor Tiberius Caesar (Fig. 14.5). He

Fig. 14.9 A copper coin of Chandragupta Vikramaditya with bare-bodied king holding bow in right hand (obverse) and the Garuda standard and illegible Sanskrit legend *Sri Vikrama* (reverse). 375–413 A.D.

was the adopted son of Augustus Caesar. His original name was Tiberius Claudius Nero, but he was often described as Tiberius Caesar Augustus or Tiberius Julius Caesar Augustus. On the obverse the portrait of the emperor was depicted with the legend TI. CLAVDIVS CAESAR, AVG. PM. TRP. IMP. Here IMP is the short form for imperator, the emperor, and PM is substituted for Pontifex Maximum, the title of the head of Roman religion which the emperor holds. Another imperial title Tribunicia Potestas is represented by TRP, which indicates that the emperor has the power of a tribune to act as the guardian of Roman Plebeians.

On most of the Roman coins the reverse has an emblem that covers the entire space, and on most of them the letters S and C appear with a little distance between them, that stand for Senatus Consulto, meaning it was issued by the decree of the Senate. Whereas on this piece most of the space is left blank except for a small indistinct symbol. Though the letter S is illegible the letter C is very clear. Measuring 3.4 cm across, it is relatively larger than most Roman coins.

Its core is made of silver while its exterior is wrapped with a foil of gold or gold alloy. Unlike most Roman coins, the Caesar's portrait and the legend are deeply

Fig. 14.10 A silver coin of Madurantaka *alias* Uttama Chola. 969–985 A.D.
Obverse: With the Nagari legend *Uttama Chola*.
Reverse: With Chola symbol of tiger, Pandya symbol of fish and Chera symbol of a bow.

Fig. 14.11 A silver coin of Vira Kerala Varman with Nagari legend. 1127 A.D.
Obverse: A crocodile moving left between the words *Sri Vira Keralasya.*

Fig. 14.12 A silver coin of Vira Kerala Varman with Nagari legend. 1127 A.D.
Reverse: A legend *Sri Gandaran Kusasya.*

engraved, but appears to have been flattened a bit by pressure. On the other hand, the other side is almost flat. All these features indicate it is an unusual coin.

During the first century AD the Indo-Roman trade was at its zenith. Historians say that the balance of trade at that time was in India's favour with the result that Romans bought Indian goods by paying in coined money, which never returned to Rome. P.T. Srinivasa Iyengar throws some light on the Roman trade with South India in his book 'History of Tamils from the earliest times to 600 AD'. Quoting from Warmington's 'Commerce between the Roman Empire and India', he tells an interesting story:

'Apparently at first a fraud was attempted to be made in the matter of exportation of coined money for "of Augustus' coins a type showing Gaius and Lucius, his adopted sons, has turned up in numbers in India and these coins are nearly always plated". Another historian "Earnest therefore thinks that they were struck especially for trade with South India where the natives (it was thought) could not as yet distinguish good Roman coins from the bad". But the Tamils proved to be too shrewd, for the experiment was not repeated by Romans.'

Yes, this piece is a plated coin. It was wrapped with a foil of gold, and its silver core is visible from the worn out parts of the exterior. These facts point to the possibility that this might be one of those fake coins brought by the Roman

Fig. 14.13 A copper coin of The Dutch United East India Company with Yanam mint mark and VOC emblem (obverse) and a Persian letter 'ain' (reverse). 1664 A.D.

traders of first century AD to South India. On the other hand this could as well be a modern imitation. In any case it is a special object of curiosity.

In two centuries of Gupta empire, the coinage was mostly in gold. In a phenomenon described as 'a rain of gold', silver and copper issues were very scarce. Only three kings, Chandra Gupta Vikramaditya, Kumara Gupta and Skanda Gupta, issued silver coins. After conquering the Saka rulers of Western region, they introduced the silver coins following the type that was in circulation. Here is an example of the silver coin of Kumara Gupta (Fig. 14.7, 14.8). The obverse has the king's portrait. Traces of corrupt Greek letters are visible behind the head of the king. On the reverse the royal symbol of Garuda is standing with outstretched wings. Around, there is a Prakrit legend in Brahmi letters: *"Parama Bhagavatha Maharajadhiraja Sri Kumara Gupta Mahendraditya'.* Kumara Gupta performed Ashvamedha Yagna and issued Ashvamedha type gold coins, which showed that he adopted the title Mahendraditya. He was compelled to issue plated coins in the home province and in Western India due to the great strain on the treasury caused by frequent wars with Pushyamitras. Skanda Gupta introduced similar silver coins for circulation in the eastern provinces, in which the Garuda symbol was replaced by a peacock.

Copper coins were issued by Samudra Gupta, Chandra Gupta Vikramaditya and Kumara Gupta. The patterns almost followed the gold and silver varieties: the reverse showed the Garuda with wings spread at the top and the name or title of the king below it. In the example shown (Fig. 14.9), the muscular body of the king without the upper garment is depicted. While most of the Gupta coins show the king holding a bow in left hand, here it is in the right hand and the arrow is in the left hand. On the reverse the Garuda emblem is prominent. A legend in Brahmi letters is faintly visible below the wing at the top. It probably reads 'Sri Vikrama'. Silver and copper coins of Guptas, being scarce, fetch higher premia in world coin auctions.

Silver coins of South Indian rulers are extremely rare, because the Southern coinage is predominated by gold or copper. A rare Chola silver coin is shown here (Fig. 14.10). This is assigned to Madurantaka *alias* Uttama Chola 969-985 AD. He is the grandson of Paranthaka (907-949 AD) and son of Gandaradhitya (956-7 AD). He assumed the title of 'Maduranthaka' (conqueror of Madura, the capital of Pandyas) in 969 AD. He adopted the title of 'Uttamachola'. He was succeeded by Raja Raja Chola in 985 AD.

On the obverse the words *'Uttama Chola'* are written in Nagari characters. On the reverse is a device that consists of the following: i) a lamp stand; ii) a stringed bow; iii) a seated tiger; iv) a vertical line; v) two upright fish; vi) all placed under an umbrella, flanked by two chamaras (fly-whisks); and vii) at the circular edge there are several decorative dots. The quality of the metal is poor, and it appears to be impure. Seated tiger is the dynastic emblem of Cholas. The emblem of fish, a Pandyan emblem, is shown in token of sovereignty over the Pandyan territory. The bow is the emblem of Cheras who were subordinate to Cholas. Similar coins were also issued by Rajendra I. This coin is extremely rare.

Vira Kerala Varman's silver coins are also very scarce. They were in circulation in Kerala during twelfth century AD (Fig. 14.11, 14.12). This silver coin has Nagari legends on both sides. On one side the name *'Sri Vira Keralasya'* is written in two lines. A crocodile moving left is seen in between the two words. On the other side is a Kalasa or Kumbha between two lines *'Sri Gandaran Kusaya'.* This is said to be the only coinage of Chera dynasty circulated in the extreme southern part of the Western coast. It is indeed very rare.

Cute little copper cash issued by the Dutch United East India company during the 17th century AD is shown here (Fig. 14.3). It appears to have been issued with the consent of Sultan Abdulla, then ruling in Golkonda. A Persian letter 'ain' is visible on one side of the coin. Above this letter a boat is depicted indicating the maritime trade of the Company. On the other side is the Company's emblem VOC that stands for the Dutch name of the Company (Vereenigde Oost Indische Compagnie). Just above these letters the mint mark 'Y' is visible, indicating that it was minted at Yanam, one of the Dutch settlements on the Eastern coast of India. Coins of Yanam mint are so rare that they were not listed in any world coin catalogues. That is what makes it a special coin.

A mint master can always create an original piece for presentation on special occasions. Sometimes the king himself or members of the royal family paid occasional visits to the mint to witness how bits of metal were being transformed into shining coins of money. On such important occasions the normal practice was to honour the visiting dignitaries with presentation of mementoes, and special coins, created for the purpose. Very rarely a separate die was cut, but it was more common to use the dies of circulation issues. By using a planchet of different metal other than the one used for regular coins, an original piece can be created.

Here is an example that was struck with the double die of a silver rupee, thus creating a copper rupee that never existed before (Fig. 14.14, 14.15). Since it was created for the purpose of presentation, it was beautified with an additional decoration. A tiny piece of gold pressed to form the letter 'C' was embedded at the centre of the coin, that stood for Calcutta Presidency of East India Company. The result was the birth of a stunning piece of incredible novelty. Since the die with Shah Alam's regnal year 20 was used by the Farukhabad mint to strike silver rupees during 1833–35, this presentation piece was probably made during that period. The existence of off-metal-strike of this kind is not yet listed in any of the world coin catalogues.

Rare coins appreciate in value like the paintings of old masters. Ancient coins of the Greek, Roman and Byzantine empires, and gold and silver coins of the world are in demand the world over. India is also a rich source of exceptionally rare coins. For example Jahangir's gold coins of zodiac series, silver coins of Gupta rulers with Sanskrit inscriptions and those of Kushana king Kanishka are considered rare. They fetch higher value in world coin auctions.

In US alone there are more than 50,000 investors who buy and sell rare coins. There are increasing number of coin dealers who look for world rarities. Single rarities from any country fetch fabulous prices. There are dealers like Ponterio & Associates in the US who are willing to travel anywhere in the world to inspect and purchase such super rarities. Three hundred year old Spink & Son Ltd. of London is famous for its dealings in world rarities. Antique dealers like Christies and Sotheby conduct regular auctions in world coin rarities. Such is the fascination the world over for these ancient artifacts.

INDEX